**NEW YORK REVIEW BOOKS**
POETS

V. R. "BUNNY" LANG (1924–1956) was a poet, playwright, actress, and director born in Boston, the youngest of six daughters. She was a founding member of the Poets' Theatre in Cambridge, Massachusetts, in 1950, where she staged two verse dramas, *Fire Exit* (1952) and *I Too Have Lived in Arcadia* (1954), and starred in multiple other productions, including the original performance of Frank O'Hara's *Try! Try!* (1951). Her poetry was widely published in her lifetime, particularly in *Poetry*, and she was, for a time, the editor of the *Chicago Review*. She died of Hodgkin's disease at the age of thirty-two.

ROSA CAMPBELL lives in Edinburgh, and is a British Academy Postdoctoral Fellow at the University of St Andrews, where she also teaches modern and contemporary literature. Her poetry has appeared in various places, including *Oxford Poetry*, *fourteen poems*, *Perverse*, *Ambit*, *Gutter*, and *SPAM*. Her first book, *Pothos*, a memoir-ish lyric essay about grief and houseplants, was published in 2021.

# *V. R. "Bunny" Lang*

# *The Miraculous Season*

## *Selected Poems*

EDITED BY ROSA CAMPBELL

**NYRB**/POETS

NEW YORK REVIEW BOOKS *New York*

THIS IS A NEW YORK REVIEW BOOK
PUBLISHED BY THE NEW YORK REVIEW OF BOOKS
207 East 32nd Street, New York, NY 10016
www.nyrb.com

*Cover and frontispiece photograph of V. R. Lang: V. R. Lang Papers, Houghton Library, Harvard, MS Am 1951 (65)*



Library of Congress Cataloging-in-Publication Data
Names: Lang, V. R., 1924–1956 author | Campbell, Rosa editor writer of introduction
Title: The miraculous season: selected poems / V. R. Lang; edited by Rosa Campbell.
Description: New York: New York Review Books, 2026. | Series: New York Review Books poets
Identifiers: LCCN 2025038219 (print) | LCCN 2025038220 (ebook) | ISBN 9798896230342 paperback | ISBN 9798896230359 ebook
Subjects: LCGFT: Poetry
Classification: LCC PS3562.A4848 M57 2026 (print) | LCC PS3562.A4848 (ebook)
LC record available at https://lccn.loc.gov/2025038219
LC ebook record available at https://lccn.loc.gov/2025038220

ISBN 979-8-89623-034-2;
Available as an electronic book; ISBN 979-8-89623-035-9

Book design adapted from a design by Andrew Latimer, Carcanet

The authorized representative in the EU for product safety and compliance is eucomply OÜ, Pärnu mnt 139b-14, 11317 Tallinn, Estonia, hello@eucompliancepartner.com, +33 757690241.

Printed in the United States of America on acid-free paper.
10 9 8 7 6 5 4 3 2 1

## *Contents*

"She is calling us long-distance in these poems, telling us how it is with her, how bright things can be, how terrible things are. She was a wonderful person. She is one of our finest poets. We are so lucky to have something of her still!"

—Frank O'Hara

# *Introduction*

*This is Miss Lang, Miss V. R. Lang. The Poet, or*
*The Poetess...   Bynum, would you introduce*
*Someone else as        this is J.P. Hatchet*
*Who is a Roman Catholic?        No. Then don't do*
*That to me again. It's not an employment,*
*It's a private religion. Who's that over there?*

You probably haven't heard of Bunny Lang. Or, if you have, it's because you're a Frank O'Hara fan, and can recall poems dedicated to her: "V. R. Lang," "An 18$^{th}$ Century Letter," "A Letter to Bunny." Or perhaps you remember the sudden shift in "A Step Away From Them," when O'Hara pivots from the joys of cheeseburgers, Coca-Cola, and hot shirtless labourers on the streets of Manhattan to the lines: "First / Bunny died, then John Latouche / then Jackson Pollock. But is the / earth as full as life was full, of them?" To learn that someone has died before you've even been introduced properly seems unfair—to you, to them. Yet this is perhaps how most people first meet V. R. "Bunny" Lang, who lived for a brief and extraordinary flash between 1924 and 1956, during which time she wrote, directed and starred in numerous plays, edited a literary magazine, co-founded the first "poets' theatre" in the United States, and wrote reams and reams of startling, fervent, visionary poetry. As O'Hara says—placing her on the same cultural pedestal as the musical theatre icon Latouche and arguably the most famous American painter of the twentieth century—"life was full" of Lang. For those that knew her, she was a "Cambridge legend of the arts," "a formidable presence," a "ball of fire."

So far, though, Lang has languished in the margins of American literary history; a footnote to the rise and rise of the New York School of poets, a curio, and—persistently—Frank

O'Hara's "muse." This is often the fate of women who happen to be connected to famous male artists and writers, regardless of their own professions or talents; relegated to the status of auxiliary, passive inspiration, they freeze into silence. The muse is not a speaking role. Yet in Lang's archives, housed at the Houghton Library at Harvard, amongst the correspondence, juvenilia, diaries, legal documents, photographs, sketches, and half-finished playscripts, there are hundreds of poems, almost all of which have lain dormant for seventy years. It turns out she had a lot to say.

Violet Ranney Lang was born in Boston on the 11th of May, 1924, the youngest of six sisters. The Langs were a well-to-do family—old money and a good name housed in a four-storey brownstone on Bay State Road, right on the Charles River. She was a debutante who was expected to marry—like her sisters did—a respectable man of her class, and settle into the life of a socialite, wife and mother. Instead, the young woman most commonly known as "Bunny" became a renegade writer and theatre impresario, gathering around her a litany of now-famous names, including Robert Bly, Harold Brodkey, Donald Hall, Mary Manning Howe, Edward Gorey, John Ashbery, Alison Lurie, Joan Mitchell, Jane Freilicher, Gregory Corso, Michael Goldberg, and—of course—Frank O'Hara.

There is a version of Lang that chimes with the expectations of her background: boarding at the Hannah More Academy; summers spent at a girls' camp in New Hampshire; formal presentation to society in 1941; member of the Vincent Club, President of the Charlotte Cushman Club. Yet this patrician litany seems to lie fundamentally at odds with some of the less conventional particulars of her life. During the Second World War, she left the University of Chicago (where she had enrolled in 1942) to join the Canadian Women's Army Corps—because the American armed forces didn't take those under 20. She went back to university for a couple of years and became editor of the *Chicago Review*, but dropped out before graduating and returned to Boston, where she moved through a string of miscellaneous jobs, often pulled from the *Help Wanted* columns: bridal consultant at Fabian Bachrach's photography studio, cosmetics demonstrator at a department store, researcher interviewing Pontiac owners, and—most infamously—burlesque dancer at the slightly seedy Old Howard Theatre. When she writes as "Anne, a Chorus Girl Quitting the Line, to Society," it's not—or not entirely—a persona. By 1949, her mother was dead and her sisters all married, but Lang continued to live with her father (the organist and piano teacher Malcolm Burrage Lang) in her once-grand childhood home, now rather shabby, the family wealth not what it once was. Here she threw parties, some "wonderful," some "terrible," housed her Siamese cats, and in her room on the top floor wrote and rewrote, typed and re-typed her poems and plays. As Nora Sayre—who knew Lang in the 1950s—writes, "she became a legend [...] a witty outlaw whose passions overflowed the confines of New England gentility." Lang was the fiery, frantic core of the Boston and Cambridge literary scene: a poet, a playwright, an actress, a director and, according to Susan Howe, "a Valkyrie." She died in 1956 of Hodgkin lymphoma; she was thirty-two.

Lang was, by all accounts, a brilliant and difficult person. Her accolades are many: "strong, opinionated, passionate," "a superb comedienne" and "overwhelmingly funny, smart, ambitious." O'Hara's friend, roommate, and sometime lover Joe LeSueur met Lang for the first time as an unannounced visitor, finding her naked in the "grimy, grayish bathtub" of their New York apartment, from which recumbent position she suggested that he make them both a drink. "I was never so quickly won over by anyone," he writes; she was "someone to reckon with and adore." Yet "formidable" is perhaps the word used most often by those that knew her. She was possessed of an "angry loyalty to everyone she accepted for her friends and lovers," but caustic in her criticism, brutal in her reprisals: "once when she felt that Ted Gorey had betrayed her she sent him a Christmas card so obscene, insulting, and spiteful that he would not speak to her for a year." At one point she became the subject of a Poets' Theatre working group to "Stop Bunny," as a result of her tendency to be overbearing and drastically over budget (she showed up at the meeting and declared them all her enemies). Once—in an anecdote that seems to typify both her incredible wrath and her impetuous creativity—she printed a thousand pink labels that read MY NAME IS STANLEY AND I AM A PIG in order to seek revenge on a man she had briefly dated, who she felt had slighted her. He found them pasted all over his New York neighbourhood; in his subway station, on the door of his apartment building, in his favourite bar, the bathrooms of his Madison Avenue office. For some time afterwards, she would sporadically send him postcards, often from abroad, the leftover labels pasted onto them. It is perhaps no surprise to find, in the middle of her poem "Address to the Redcoats," Paul Gauguin's maxim: "*Life / Being what it is, one dreams of revenge.*"

In 1946, one of the first classes of Second World War veterans descended on Cambridge to attend Harvard on the GI Bill. Among them was a young man in a Navy workshirt who would later become one of the brightest stars in the constellation known as the New York School. It would be easy to suggest that Frank O'Hara, with his current status as a cult icon of American poetry, must have been a significant influence on his now lesser-known friend. At the time, however, O'Hara was an aspiring musician, focused on piano concertos and Elementary Harmony, whilst Lang was in possession of relative local fame and a much more established literary career; she had already been the editor of the *Chicago Review*, and her poems had been published by *Poetry*, *i.e. The Cambridge Review*, and *Folder*. Indeed, Lang's reputation clearly preceded her; seeing her for the first time at a bookstore cocktail party, O'Hara remembered that "as if it were a movie, she was glamorous and aloof. The girl I was talking to said: 'That's Bunny Lang. I'd like to give her a good slap.'" They became inseparable.

It was together that Lang and O'Hara worked out how to be poets. O'Hara recalled how they "sounded each other out for hours over beers, talking incessantly," and argued over influences: "We both loved Rimbaud and Auden; she thought I loved Rimbaud too much, and I thought the same about Auden and her." It was an intense and symbiotic relationship, sustained by their shared unwavering commitment to poetry and a potent sibling-like bond (a letter from Lang to O'Hara greets him as "Brother," while another is addressed to "Trick" and signed "Treat"). The two poets began a routine of "coffee talks," daily telephone calls to talk about "everything we had thought of since we had parted the night before, including any dreams we may have had in the meantime." At the top of the Bay State Road house, according to O'Hara's biographer Brad Gooch, they "sat together writing joke poems, collaborating on alternate lines, or correcting each other's work so that it was difficult to tell whose was whose." Indeed, Lang's poem "To Frank's Guardian Angel" was mistakenly included in the first edition of O'Hara's *Collected Poems*, after being found by Kenneth Koch, Bill Berkson, and other friends tasked with collating his poems after he died in 1966. Perhaps if Koch et al had seen the original title of the poem, they might not have been so sure it was O'Hara's; instead of the seemingly self-reflexive naming gesture evident elsewhere in O'Hara's work ("Some day I'll love Frank O'Hara," he writes in the poem "Katy"), another draft of the poem sports the rather more teasing title "To the Guardian Angel of an Aesthete Going to the Middle West to College." Critics have occasionally used this editorial mishap to suggest that Lang, therefore, must necessarily have been influenced by, and sound like, O'Hara. It is too simplistic a rebuttal to suggest that O'Hara perhaps sounds like Lang; each was, of course, a reverberation of the other. We could, however, turn to Bill Corbett, who claimed that the renowned New York School poet Bernadette Mayer's response to reading Lang's work was "I like her poems better than O'Hara's."

It wasn't just Lang and O'Hara, however. Robert Bly, another Harvard student at the time, described a coterie made up of "an astonishing collection of intense maniacs," often crowded into a booth at Jim Cronin's bar on Dunster Street, with Lang holding court as "the Circe of that circle." This group included Lyon Phelps, George Montgomery, Hugh Amory, Sarah Braveman, Hal Fondren, Lawrence Osgood and—later—Gregory Corso, who would go on to be a major poet of the Beat Generation. Lang had met him penniless in New York and brought him back to Cambridge, insisting that he be moved into Peter Sourian's room in Harvard's Eliot House, and given a job sweeping the newly-established Poets' Theatre. It was this theatre that formed the hub of the New England literary scene at mid-century. In 1950, together with Mary Manning (Molly) Howe (mother of the poets Fanny and Susan Howe), Thornton Wilder, and Lyon Phelps, Lang co-founded the theatre, with the support and blessing of the town's poetic grandees, Richard Eberhart, John Ciardi, and Richard Wilbur. An experiment in medium, form, and organisation, the Poets' Theatre was to become a significant testing ground for young writers, actors, artists and designers, prefiguring the Artists' Theatre, set up in 1953 in New York by John Bernard Myers and Herbert Machiz (who would later stage Lang's *Fire Exit* in 1954), and the New York Poets Theatre, which was founded in 1961 by a group of poets including Amiri Baraka (then LeRoi Jones) and Diane di Prima.

Originally holding the position of Secretary, and later becoming Vice-President, Lang was the only founding member of the theatre to have no formal connection to Harvard. Yet as Don Share points out, she "was surpassed—slightly—in her publishing record only by the senior members of the theatre, Richard Wilbur, John Ciardi, and Richard Eberhart." All of the theatre's early productions featured Lang as writer, director, or actor, or occasionally all three. The Poets' Theatre was more than a workshop for writers trying their hand at verse drama; it saw itself as the vanguard of an innovation in American literature. It was also a crucible for gossip, feuds, and vendettas—both artistic and personal. It was DIY, underground, and often broke—no thanks to Lang, who had been known to run up colossal debts for her productions. Shows could involve Victorian gothic sets by Edward Gorey and strange costumes hand-dyed by Lang in her basement, while actors bickered over the casting of roles; it had an air of "intentional delinquency." Yet it also had lofty ambitions that were realised with surprising frequency; original works by Samuel Beckett, Cid Corman, and Ted Hughes were staged there; it hosted the first American reading by Dylan Thomas of *Under Milk Wood*; and the first reading of Djuna Barnes's play *The Antiphon* took place in Lang's sister-in-law's Berkeley Street mansion, attended by Robert Lowell, Elizabeth Hardwick, Edwin Muir, I. A. Richards, and—somewhat astonishingly—T. S. Eliot, whom Lang, never one to be overawed, had personally invited. Yet Nora Sayre remembers that "above all, the company had an exciting aura of a counterculture, which was very hard to locate in the Fifties."

Echoes of the Poets' Theatre—and poetic drama more generally—can be seen throughout Lang's poetry. Not just in poems like "Whisper," "I give you my wheel and my skate," and "Lines for Mrs C," which are composed as dialogues (or, in the case of the last, a monologue with accompanying cat-yowls), but also in the declarative grandstanding of poems such as "Address to the Redcoats," which was written to be delivered as part of a reading in May 1954, not long after Lang had been diagnosed with Hodgkin lymphoma. Alison Lurie describes how she arrived to give the reading "looking ghastly pale and haggard, dressed in low-cut black velvet like Madame Bovary." Elsewhere in her work, Lang creates high drama and spectacular characters, so that we are swept up in the theatre of a poem like "Pique-Dame"—courts and assassins and Ice Lakes and "every tree breaking"—before we register that "Pique-Dame" is the Queen of Spades and lines like "Pique-Dame, I am losing. / Save me, and I will play you" could be read entirely literally as a card game. On the other hand, it is difficult to let such mundanity get in the way of the invocation of Calliope (the muse of epic poetry), and the way the poem explodes itself by the end, bursting outwards into teeming chaos:

> EVERYONE UP          EVERYTHING
> VERY LOUD AND BEAUTIFUL   crying red and yellow
> Calliope, calliope      every tree breaking
> Ponds leaping wild      wheels        trees bracelets birds
> The plums are wild      with what is coming
> Everything a Wonder          all open hands
> Listen!      you've got to listen      PIQUE-DAME! PIQUE-DAME!

The movement in "Pique-Dame" from tight lines and traditional conceit to an eruption of fragmentary, impressionistic, semi-surrealist modernity is a reflection of the range of Lang's writing more generally, something this selection aims to reveal. By experiencing her work as an oeuvre—albeit a necessarily incomplete one—the true breadth of Lang's accomplishment becomes apparent. She is as good at pith ("Heard at the P.O.: Hate. Nobody likes their mail") as she is at pathos ("I think I die within the year"), as skilled a formalist ("Surprise Party") as she is an experimentalist (["excuses, excuses"]). In this, she perhaps does take after Auden, her greatest poetic love, matching his ability to shift from dramatic monologue to light verse to prose poem, without sacrificing an integral voice. Often, Lang's range appears in a single poem, such as the one beginning "With all these justifiable fears that I may cease to be / I'm living upside down," in which the roguish candour gives way to a kind of pop nonsense verse—"It's up to You / To do / The Hachacha. / Only You / Can do / The Hachachacha"—before pulling us up short at the end: "And only You / Can call the dogs back." Such vicissitudes can also be seen in "Discredited Things," a poem of superstition and magic that invokes the Norns—the Norse giantess-gods of fate—alongside indistinct "Spirits" and "powers" and unnameable (but capitalised) "Things." The world it conjures is one in which "stones see back" and everything from "water" to "public Parks" "All go secretly, knowingly on." Yet when you come to read this poem, it may not feel quite as uncanny as you expect, because it's prefaced with the incongruously banal epigraph: "'The tongue is a great magnifier, Mrs DuBois' — My sister's dentist." It is perhaps no surprise that she is reported to have "nettled" John Ashbery by telling him he took art too seriously.

The experience of reading Lang's poems is often one of astonishment, whether from the cumulative experience of the breadth of her vision, or the eye-watering acidity of a single phrase. Her endings, in particular, have a tendency to knock the wind out of a reader (it would not do justice to these moments to quote lines in isolation; I hope you find yourself winded occasionally as you read). Part of this general air of surprise stems from the work's resistance to categorisation. Like many twentieth-century women, she has been occasionally and half-heartedly co-opted into some of the major movements of the time. Is there something Beat-esque about poems like "American Idealism," with its "pop pop," "bang bang" interjections, its run-on (and prophetic?) declarations of a generational identity ("We are the chopjaw draftcard bonfires")? Is there a New York School urban pastoral vision in the image of a "springing Botticelli lawn / Down Fiftyseventh Street"? Perhaps (although there is also something slightly skewed and outsidery in her rendering of "Fiftyseventh" as opposed to "57th"). Lang *could* be seen as a stone in the architecture of these towering avant-gardes, as part of an overlooked generation of mid-century women poets, or as the rightful heir to Wallace Stevens and W.H. Auden (though the latter outlived her, in the end). But really she is a kind of singularity; more interested in archaism than Ginsberg or Corso, angrier and more melodramatic than Ashbery or O'Hara, funnier than Laura Riding, stranger in phrase and image than Rosalie Moore, and possessed of a rawness difficult to locate in Auden or Stevens. Throughout, her poetry eludes a definable aesthetic, and instead returns and returns to a state of perversity and defiance.

Lang's work has what Maggie Nelson has called an "intentional awkwardness," and such brass-necked writing could also be seen to have a certain class inflection; the same entitlement that enabled her to be "constantly praising or criticizing everyone's poems," and to be given, for *Fire Exit*, "a budget larger than that of any previous production, yet which Bunny considered to be an insult," giving rise to a poetic voice that feels dauntless and assured. This voice is truculent, unyielding, and occasionally pugnacious, but often deliciously, viciously funny ("Suicide Note" features the pitiless yet drily recognisable sentiment, "I wish you no petty dismays, I wish you a lingering curse").

It would be too easy to tie anecdotes such as the one about Stanley and the pig labels to poems like that which begins

"Rage, but a degenerate rage," in which anger manifests itself as "Taking from innocent particulars / Motive, mood, vengeance." Yet there is a playfulness evident in both—the ludicrous extravagance of the thousand pink labels chimes with the poem's refusal to indulge in misery. The pathos of thwarted desires ("I will never go there now") is undercut by a frankly camp dismissal of the Dardanelles as one of "the bargain paradises." Such subversion is a hallmark of Lang's work. She endlessly shifts and pivots between sincerity and irony, conversationalism and melodrama.

She also has a pastoral mode that swings between the darkly surreal (as in the image of the "leaves that choked me" in "Who strained this fuzzy air") and the idyllic and arcadian: "All that summer we lived in a cabin / By a white agile brook specked with sun," she writes in "We passed by the irrelevant echo," "We called to imagined bears, we were their keepers." Nature, for Lang, is often secretive and mysterious, enfolding itself around human incident, as at the end of "A Sunday Indignity," in which the profound indifference of the natural world conspires with the poet to keep us from truly bearing witness:

> She screamed, but the river ran on and along
> With the running of the day, the ripple of water rushes,
> The upwards cluttered struggle of the growing roses,
> The stillness of the secret sun.

The poem resonates with echoes of Auden's "Musée des Beaux Arts" and its central thesis on suffering: "how it takes place / While someone else is eating or opening a window or just walking dully along." Where, though, in Auden's poem, "everything turns away / Quite leisurely from the disaster" of Icarus' fall, Lang's is laced with a horror that is simultaneously weirder and more earthly; the strange attackers, "squat like tubers, undersoil," who "closed in around her" are—prosaically—"boys."

On a rare hot day on the east coast of Scotland, I had my own mysterious meeting of the human and natural. Printouts of Lang's poems were strewn all over the floor—perhaps mimicking the stacks of "papers, papers" and "unmailed letters" that populate the poems themselves—and I was ordering and re-ordering, second-guessing, wondering what she would want. Suddenly, through the open window and straight to the top of a bookcase, flew a small bird, who sat chirruping and reshuffling his feathers. "He isn't a bird like the birds I've known," writes Lang, "And I've been places, and I've seen birds." If her poems are anything to go by, she's right: birds appear throughout, from "municipal swans" in the Public Gardens to sparrows being fed watermelon, "Scraping the exhausted rind with a spoon", to the "disinterested nearness" of a pigeon audience in Fogg Court, where some early Poets Theatre productions were staged. They are the prey of cats and they burst from closets, they are vocal, shrieking or singing or in some kind of conversation with the poet. They can be augurs—"sparrows falling and dying"—or personally threatening: "Only in silence the crow in the corner / Stares at my performance, makes me make / Mistakes." In particular, white birds show up regularly—a "white hawk," a white "chicken feather." But most ubiquitous is the recurrent enigma of the white crow, to which Lang returns over multiple poems. In "To Frank's Guardian Angel," "Crows fly white," while "25 Years" features a "day of the white crow," yet the symbolism of this image for Lang seems murky. In the poem that treats it most fully, "[I waited five hundred centuries for the White Crow]," an entire three-act narrative is relayed in the second line alone, shot through with expectant caesuras: "I waited      IT CAME      IT FLEW AWAY." These lacunae are perhaps the only explanation we can expect from Lang, cagey as she often is—gaps waiting for readers to fill them. The bird that visited me in my office was not a white crow, but something small and brown and friendly. I didn't have any watermelon on hand, and in the end, it too flew away.

The last person to be faced with the task of transforming Lang's sprawling oeuvre into a book was Bradley Sawyer Phillips, the Cambridge-born painter to whom she was married for the final year of her life. As her literary executor, he worked tirelessly from very soon after her death to gain Lang further publication and recognition, finally in 1962 selecting and editing the self-published collection *The Pitch*, carrying out the bulk of the editorial work with Lang's friends and fellow writers Lawrence Osgood and Mac Hammond (superseding her own appointment of Helen Wells, Julia Randall, and an as-yet unidentified "Steph" as literary advisors). Featuring forty eight poems and the playscripts of *Fire Exit* and *I Too Have Lived in Arcadia*, *The Pitch* would later be fused with Alison Lurie's memoir of Lang to be published with Random House in 1975 as *V. R. Lang: Poems & Plays with a Memoir by Alison Lurie*. This is long out of print and hard to come by, and Lurie's introductory memoir (which takes up almost a third of the book), though full of lively anecdotes, seems to regard Lang's actual writing as second order. Heartfelt but frivolous, Lurie's account of Lang reads as part-eulogy, part-gossip column, and is often less than flattering about its subject (rather bizarrely, it opens with a description of Lang's "firm, fair, heavy flesh"). A small *New York Times* review at the time described it as a piece "where resentment and affection are [...] thoroughly mixed." It is perhaps no wonder that Lang's poetic star twinkled out after her death.

Phillips's editorial approach seems to be fairly accurately summarised in a letter he sent to Angus Fletcher at *i.e. The Cambridge Review* in 1956 upon Fletcher's rejection of some of Lang's work, posthumously submitted:

> The implication in your letter and in our conversation that I was attempting to fob off some fragments onto you is infuriating. I certainly would not permit anything of Bunny's that I did not consider finished and admirable to be published anywhere, even in a magazine of as small a circulation as yours.

This is extremely telling, showcasing not only Phillips's dedication to establishing Lang as a writer of consequence, but also his sense of what kind of work might achieve that status—'finished and admirable.' During the process of editing her work for possible publication, Phillips, Osgood and Hammond marked up versions of Lang's poems into a number of categories, designating them "EARLY DRAFT," "ONLY DRAFT," and "FINAL DRAFT." It is unclear from these documents what criteria were used to classify those marked "FINAL DRAFT," but it's evident that they leaned towards drafts that were shorter, more formally strict, less enjambed and had titles. The opening and title poem, "The Pitch," for example, is a nine-stanza poem in all of the available drafts, as well as in its publication in *Poetry* in 1950; in *The Pitch*, however, two of the middle stanzas—more violent in their imagery—were removed. The three men also often added punctuation, particularly commas and full-stops to the end of lines and poems, a convention that truncates Lang's writing and presents her as a much more formal poet than she appears in her own drafts.

Some of the many things I have regrettably had to leave out of this book are the fragments that litter the files of Lang's archive. They are handwritten in pencil on little blue sheets and scribbled in the margins of theatre programmes, typed on the torn-off top of a letter draft or hovering speculatively at the bottom of the manuscript of a poem. Sometimes these are lines that will later be found, properly aligned in the middle of a page, a poem built around them, while others hang, like visions or aphorisms, suspended without scaffolding in uncertain white space. One such fragment appears on yet another sheet of tissuey paper, sandwiched between various typed and handwritten shards of poetry and catty comments, and reads:

> Let the unfinished masterpieces hang over your life
> Like a creeping shadow, let the waiting silence
> Steal all of your pains and your patience

Except that "unfinished" is handwritten in pencil over the top of a crossed-out word. In the Houghton Library, I hold the page up to the sunlight spilling in from Harvard Yard, and make out that the original word was "ungoverned." There is something unbearably poignant about these lines, which are impossible to read now without thinking of the truncated life of their author—meteoric in its truest sense, burning painfully bright, and flaming out. Her ambitions not fully realised and her star only half-risen, Bunny Lang had unfinished business.

Yet what is most interesting in these lines is actually precisely that shift from "ungoverned" to "unfinished," an edit that suggests a kind of equivalence between these two concepts. In Lang's mind, perhaps, to be ungoverned *is* to be unfinished—to write unfinished work is to refuse governance. For me, these are not lines of resignation, but of defiance. If a sense of unfinishedness permeates Lang's legacy, it is not just because of the tragedy of her early death, but also that her poems engage with a sense of deliberate incompletion, unafraid to allow for hazy imagery, disjointed syntax, wavering speakers, and frequent interruptions. In "Poems to Preserve the Years at Home," she writes, "*Not to finish* becomes the challenge," a sentiment particularly apt for a poem that seems to be unbounded by time (undefined "Years" in an undefined "Home") or by length, its collage of sections spooling out with the promise of perpetuity. This is a poem of inconstancy and inconclusiveness: "Everything begun. Nothing ever finished. / Heaps and piles of waste." These "heaps and piles of waste" seem to mirror the poem itself, the "boxes, papers, papers, drawers / Files… filing cabinets… especial drawers" of poems pulled together to "preserve" a life. Anxiety about mortality permeates the sequence, as "Time grows thin," but it is not a fear of leaving things incomplete. Instead, a fierce commitment to ongoingness is the real driving force.

Like many New York School poets, Lang chronicles the creation of the poem, including the extraneous impositions that prevent it from becoming "finished" or polished: "The typewriter which jams. The voice downstairs / That calls. The telephone which enters." She aligns the material obstacles to writing—"Can't make two letters come together right / On this damnable machine"—with the intellectual or aesthetic ones, rendering them of equal importance, so that the process and "point" of the poem is "Bewildering. Complicated. Preferably / Mysterious to the self at the time of writing."

For Lang, unfinishedness constitutes a form of refusal, so that "*Not to finish*" suggests not only an acceptance of incoherence and incompletion, but also a defiance of endings that echoes the other disobediences and subversions of expectation seen in both her work and life. Nora Sayre notes that "wherever she operated, Bunny seemed to personify a world of cultural rebellions; her intimates fondly called her a subversive." "Poems to Preserve the Years at Home," as it appears in this volume, is a manifestation of that defiance, in that it gathers up a much wider range of work than appears in *The Pitch* and *Poems & Plays*. In its previously published version, this poem is just as beautiful, but not as raw—it appears as a much tighter, nine-poem sequence, with Phillips making a selection from a list of poems touted for inclusion. By contrast, presented with this list as part of the selection process for *The Pitch*, Frank O'Hara simply ticked the heading "Poems to Preserve the Years at Home," indicating that everything under it should be included. Indeed, in a letter to Larry Osgood at the time, he made clear his editorial views:

> Bunny and I often discussed the thing about "finished" and "unfinished" poems, to the effect that we both felt that the poem sometimes finished itself before we realized it or before we had wanted it to [...] Sometimes the dissatisfaction which leads one to put something away for a few weeks and look at it later is not that the work is unfinished, but the inspiration is unfinished. You look at it later and realize that it is complete, and meanwhile the dissatisfaction has disappeared because it was part of the occasion rather than real critical response. It would be a shame if the poems that she had "given up" on were excluded.

It is O'Hara's approach that I have tried to channel in making this selection of Lang's work—along with that slippage between *unfinished* and *ungoverned*. I've tried to govern as little as possible: where her poems are untitled, they remain so; where Phillips, Osgood and Hammond wanted to add punctuation, her lines survive uncurtailed. Separate poems with the same title are included as pairs, yoked by Lang's recursive tendency, and her own alternative titles are given in brackets. Her idiosyncrasy of rendering "each other" as "eachother" is retained. "Poems to Preserve the Years at Home" is let loose as the magnum opus it deserves to be. So too does her work refuse the governance of time; almost all of Lang's papers are undated, so there is no chronology in this selection—just some (bird-assisted) sense of relationships and narrative; a little bit of poets theatre.

These may or may not be the right editorial choices, but I am less interested in presenting a definitive version of Lang's poetry than in revivifying it, opening up each poem and agitating its surface once again, after too long left in "waiting silence." Lang clearly wrote poems her whole life; in her archive, early works populate the pages of childhood diaries, alongside inky sketches of strange beaky figures, and significant teenage plans ("The next pgs are devoted to the personal improvement of Jean, Ethel & Violet. […] P.S. Violet did not improve. Neither Jean or Ethel. P.P.S. Jean, in time, did get better looking"). Despite her lifelong devotion to writing, however, the body of work presented here is really a kind of flash, spanning less than fifteen years even at its outer edges, the greatest part of it written between 1948 and 1956.

In 2009, the Brooklyn-based artist Spencer Finch (another bird!) created an installation of 366 paraffin candles, arranged in a spiral on a gallery floor. Every day for a year, a new candle was lit and burned down, spreading coloured wax into its neighbour. The piece was a visual representation of 1892, Emily Dickinson's *annus mirabilis*—miraculous year—in which she wrote 366 poems in 365 days. In the poem that closes and titles this book, Lang writes not of a miraculous year, but "the miraculous season." This is perhaps how we can best view her writing life; an all-too-brief spell of extraordinary time, incandescent with candlelight. It has, somehow, been a hundred years since she was born, but here she is, handing you a match.

*Rosa Campbell, 2023*
*(revised 2026)*

# *Notes*

"She is calling us" (epigraph): Frank O'Hara, *Standing Still and Walking in New York* (Grey Fox Press, 1983), 88

"First / Bunny died": Frank O'Hara, 'A Step Away from Them,' *The Collected Poems of Frank O'Hara* (University of California Press, 1995), 257

"Cambridge legend": Bill Corbett, "Notes on Bunny Lang," *SpoKe 4* (2017), 221

"a formidable presence": Nora Sayre, "The Poets' Theatre: A Memoir of the Fifties," *Grand Street*, Vol.3, No.3 (1984), 100

"ball of fire": Susan Howe, "Bunny: Susan Howe on V. R. Lang," Clocktower Radio (2004)

"wonderful"; "terrible": Alison Lurie, *V. R. Lang: Poems & Plays with a Memoir by Alison Lurie* (Random House, 1975), 4

"she became a legend": Nora Sayre, 101

"a Valkyrie": Susan Howe

"strong, opinionated": Susan Howe

"a superb comedienne": Nora Sayre, 100

"overwhelmingly smart": Susan Howe

"grimy, grayish bathtub": Joe LeSueur, *Digressions on Some Poems by Frank O'Hara* (Farrar, Straus and Giroux, 2003), 36

"angry loyalty": Lurie, 6

"once when she felt": Lurie, 59

"Stop Bunny": Lurie, 25

"as if it were a movie"; "sounded each other out"; "We both loved": O'Hara, *Standing Still and Walking in New York*, 86

"Brother"; "Trick"; "Treat": V. R. Lang, V. R. Lang Papers, MS Am 1951, Houghton Library, Harvard (16); (90)

"everything we had thought": O'Hara, *Standing Still and Walking in New York*, 86 “sat together”: Brad Gooch, *City Poet: The Life and Times of Frank O’Hara* (Harper Perennial, 2014), 149

“Katy”: O’Hara, *Collected*, 242

“I like her poems”: Bill Corbett, 224

“an astonishing collection”: Robert Bly in Gooch, 148–49

“was surpassed”: Don Share, “Don Share on V. R. ‘Bunny’ Lang,” *Kenning Editions* (2010)

“intentional delinquency”: Nora Sayre, 98

“above all”: Nora Sayre, 98

“looking ghastly pale”: Lurie, 51–52

“nettled”: John Ashbery, letter to O’Hara (1950) in Gooch, 162

“intentional awkwardness”: Maggie Nelson, *Women, The New York School, and Other True Abstractions* (University of Iowa Press, 2007), 64

“constantly praising”: Gooch, 162

“a budget”: Lurie, 25

“firm, fair, heavy flesh”: Lurie, 3

“where resentment”: Sallie Bingham, “V. R. Lang,” *New York Times* (October 26, 1975)

“The implication”: Bradley Phillips, letter to Angus Fletcher (1956), V. R. Lang Papers, MS Am 1951, Houghton Library, Harvard (130)

“wherever she operated”: Nora Sayre, 102

“Bunny and I”: O’Hara, letter to Larry Osgood (1956) in Gooch, 286–87

“The next pgs”: V. R. Lang, diary entry (October 13, undated), V. R. Lang Papers, MS Am 1951, Houghton Library, Harvard (18)

*The Miraculous Season*

## *[Darling, they have discovered Dynamite]*

Darling, they have discovered Dynamite,
What do you think of that.
One day, asleep in our bed
            isolated save where our hands met
Each trying to take the blanket,
Subversive, sullen, in poor health
But safe, safe to regret
And bewail and betray and to meet
At meals with vindictive eyes
We were hopeless and we were
Shapeless but we lived with manners
And we held up our ends.
We could remember better neighbors,
We pretended we didn't mind
That the street where we lived had no trees
Or that our children didn't seem to honour us
We had the cracked cup and the cracked plate
We did not enjoy what we ate
We hated our neighbors and knew them to be worthless
But that was before they discovered dynamite.
Now we will never be so happy again.

## *[Darling, they have discovered Dynamite]*

Darling, they have discovered Dynamite,
This is it.

Yesterday we slept without it
Tonight we have to think about it.

# *Already Ripening Barberries Are Red*

"Already ripening barberries grow red,
the ageing asters scarce breathe in their bed.
Who is not rich, with summer nearly done,
will never have a self that is his own..."
Rainer Maria Rilke, *Book of Hours*, tr. Babette Deutsch

1.
This time was very like the last time,
A metaphor would do as well:
A stranger bathing in the sea survived a snail,
The real could not compete with the original.
Through these revivals I have held to one idea,
I have had it well or ill—

As large as life (my own), for reference—not knowing
Exactly what it is, but it is All.
Yesterday I drove four miles to get the mail,
Today I lie here going bad, you know I can.

The sun leaves the beach like the tide itself,
Washed out like water, soda-bright and mineral—
Sinks to the sand grass, then breaks fall
To sit above me on the dunes. I lay awake all day.
I stared at a burnt match six feet away
Stiff at my feet like a scarecrow's spine.
So by a buried animal
Sometimes a stick will stand, without his name.

2.

Seen at the beaches: stones. As various as profane.
Feet go back to whence they came.
Shins go back to knees and knees go Home.

I told you once, you have forgotten it,
How gulls from this island go at sunset
With the ferry to the inward islands, spend the night,
Return the next day or the next, indifferent
To where they were or will be, but expedient.
Just turning back to fly here with the morning boat.

Or so a day
We went to one of those bars.
There's nothing else to do at night here
Except the summer theatre
Or bathing in the bay
Or just to sit on porches, looking at the fog.
On Pentecost, I think it was,
A dog I patted bit me in the leg.
The people with me burst out laughing.
Nothing since to write that is amusing.

3.
My head is bleached, the casing too.
I feel it beating when I shut my eyes.
I think the innocent may meet in Paradise
And speak together, still and blue.
I'll not meet you.
Children shall, who race and stamp on beaches,
Whose cries go out to sea. They are themselves sea creatures—
Hard outside and soft in through.
They have no tongues for talking like we do.
If they should die

Before they go back to the mainland after Labor Day,
They would I know still speak together, still and blue.
We have no tongues for talking like they do.

Our fantastic bones bite inward and unseen,
Not sanded like a child's not salty and not dry,
Not open to the wind, not bleached by sun.
Our flesh is all apparent.
                                        Our Selves are done and known.
They lie behind us pointing to the land.
The lists are taken and the weather done,
The letters written and the mailboat gone.
What we are is known by some.
                                        Others need not guess
Wherever we applied for permits or paid taxes,
We left reports of our engagement.

That time was wasted in the search for home:
Returning inland touched with sun,
I can watch the gulls without resentment.

4.

                                        Oh, so.
Heard at the P.O.: Hate. Nobody likes their mail.
Even the mothers of sons grow weak and spoil.
"I wanted a dog—" one wept, I heard her cry.
Or a white hawk, or a shark. That was July.

Time enough to compromise, when weather will not fail;
Now the circuits spark and grab, that later will be cool.
Light can come
Only, I know at six in summer,
From what is dumb.

I will find the mirror image later, falling from
Bridges to bridge beneath.
Fountains, then, in quiet shows,
Equestrian statues,
In reflection come to faith
Crookedly contained in
Lines bent in from the horizon.

The sun makes bad.
Never so whole or well,
I climb to deeper than I can to sleep.
All I know is all I keep.
Someday, not today, I'll write you.

## *[Lately by language]*

Lately by language,
What broke I wonder, some heat I touched by,
Some stealing summer where

Greens overwhelmed the fall
Made havoc of the sleeping stones, sprang
Wild about the well.

A childhood lay behind us like an iron spring,
Some season lay beyond us like a stain,
When the river caught between us as a slate burned scar

Splashed up as we stood distant from eachother
And washed away like light, there was no longer
Anything between us but a locked surprise

Which watched the struggling rushes, heard
The shrieking birds, then fell about our feet.
We crossed. The light flew overhead.

Vines climbed up and everywhere we stood,
Until, afraid, we thrust them back, and turned
From the empty river, now grown tall and loud,
small animals rioting in its bed.

## *[Well this is another city]*

Well this is another city
Better nor worse but different
You asked how I was, I'm different
You asked if I'm well, I am

Snow came trailing disorder
Chewed all over with dirt remaining snow
Speckles the city, that's no different
But that a different time the vision

Was whiter, no bigger than I was
I saw white and tangled with nothing
That I could not know or break. Listen,
I couldn't have kept that comfort, certainty.

## *The Pitch*

Spring you came marvellous with possibles
Marvels sparked everywhere burning from bracken
Lichen leapt crackling, and long grass

And everywhere my feet went the ground swung up giddy
Green and joy-panicked, then winter went under wonder
Sun stormed white furious skies where we went running

Then nothing I touched that didn't burst out into flames,
Nothing I cried out that didn't catch fire,
Nothing I called that didn't know its name

Then all the aisles of light the streets led somewhere
I streaked down never scaring or looking backwards
At nowhere behind me go small.

Summer I saw from a tree where I hung by my neck
Caught up and hidden by vines, but I saw everything
By all my senses violent by pain.

The only marvellous the storms and they were marvellous
And I shrieked back above them cracked wide open
*Why not*, when birds escaping cried to me, *you strangle*

But in the fall the earth fell and I followed
Fell and dropped me into darkness like a death
Where I shut out and dull and dour and tacit

Itched in the creeping stone that ate my flesh,
Until in stone I stumbled, wandered,
Found a company that like me knew no wonder

But voiceless, weary, monolithic, walked around
An underground of seasons where the light like pain
Twitched where it touched us, and flaked down

## *[You didn't mail the letters]*

You didn't mail the letters that began,
"I am ashamed for both of us", didn't write
The letter that began, "I pity you. But I am hopeless."
We didn't write. We let others tell us
Where we were and what we could expect of life
That would surround us while we went doggedly on
Insisting we were not what we were,
That we had not done what we had done,
That nothing but good could come of bad,
Or even, that we had written a letter saying
"I am desperately sorry, I would rather have
Loved you than fallen to disgrace, than needed
To degrade us both and hold you as contemptuous
In everything I said from that time on..."
And mailed it, mailed it with at least that
Final generosity of spirit. But rather, we
Took poison and were poisoned. Lived to say
"I was mistaken." Lived to say, "It was nothing."
And, "I am faultless." When we lived misshapen.

## *Nantucket After Dark*

It was until six o'clock
So bright with light the figures dazzled
And vision trembled with too much, a tear
Blurred everything by caressing the wound
That the sun touched...

Then went to change their costume
The couple from Whitefish Bay, the gay
Assorted frolickers from somewhere in Missouri
And their dog

Haberdashers,
Someone who lavishes upon interiors
Follicled walls, broken columns, nudes
In darting fancies for living-rooms
The waiters plan to photograph each other
On the beach tomorrow, the sun squats down
To some flats at the sea's edge

Baby, here your tiny hand
In mine the moist reminder
That grand blue jade barbaric sea
Is not the same on land

Night is not day and never was
Night is not day and never has
(The light is different, for us)
Day is not night and never does

## *Eurydice to Orpheus*

I *wanted* him to look at me.
It meant the end of the world, but I wanted it,
It meant the sky's drop and the earth's derision,
Swallowing me from the light forever, but I willed him
To look at me and lose me, lest he forget to mourn me,
Lest he hold me ever less than that moment, a terror,
A desolation, not anything else again ever mattering.

## *Two Cats Have Killed a Bird*

*For Frank O'Hara*

We lay fat cats in a meadow under a milkweed sky,
Still from the thrush, the circling crow, the dragon-fly,

Incurious, complaisant, drunk with heat.
*What did we do, how did we live before we met*

*Our Variety?* Once, we could have done with One,
Before we learned the claw's design,

Before the needles of the tongue
Learned to strike the spine! Then,

Did the fur creep for a fire further
Than the skulking lover, later, could come?

Then, if we could touch eachother,
Could we eat together? Was everything the same?

The lizard leaps from us! The cuckoo died
With a queer, bold cry!

Now there are Three—to kill, to keep, to claim—
We cannot lie with all of them.

## *[Here in rehearsal]*

Here in rehearsal, the miracle lease
Of the happy time

The broken candlestick of four, we use it still,
Barometers and clocks that, useless on the wall,
Are passionately needed in the ritual

Recall, recall, and sang the white birds past never
Early over the morning, by the immobile tree

Why must the river change constantly behind us?
Why all traffic over these bridges flow and renew?
Our clocks stand fixed, no hour strikes together,
Lamps some unlit some long ago patient stare stand still

These were the things we bought, the way we dressed;
Now when these precious break they are not replaced,
Now guests no longer come here to dismay our waiting

## *Discredited Things (Waiting and Peeking)*

"The tongue is a great magnifier, Mrs DuBois"
—My sister's dentist

Nobody believes in Fate anymore, nobody listens to the Norns.
Nobody solicits garlic and white of egg, or fears effigies.
But Things go on anyway, arranging everything that happens.

People think unkindly of others, and these in particular
Break out in horrible rashes, or die in convulsions.
Spirits sift and creep, and stones see back.

Trees and rocks and water and public Parks
All go secretly, knowingly on, and every quiet, heavy Thing
Maintains its own life and its powers, peeking at us as it does.

## *[Girl, what a song you were]*

Girl, what a song you were
When wild poppies cast gold at your feet
And you stepped on a springing Botticelli lawn
Down Fiftyseventh Street.

Unsorrowing, unbarred melody
Abiding nobody's questions
The workaday webs of us admiring spiders
Hampered your progressions

We must have been deaf when we tried to whistle the tune
Smothered the song and somehow lost the key –
The echo still sounds somewhere, paler now,
In its gay, and lonely, proud insanity.

That you were beautiful I'll testify
How well you walked I know
I'll look down Fiftyseventh Street a long time
To see wild poppies grow.

## *[I waited all that time for a bird I wanted]*

I waited all that time for a bird I wanted.
In a bucket of limestone. Taking form
Like a diamond only a little more lively
The zone was horror. I stayed within the bounds.
It took place like five hundred centuries
Barely heaving. Shifting into folds and faults—
Zones and vaults. *It will come*, I said,
My strength locked up in order to endure
So that I spoke in frozen sounds, barely a whisper
It will come from that slight overture now
Overhead apparent in the mine
Wounds of the deep dead: do not bleed,
Crack and flake, shrink down
Early Monday morning we arise without echo
I learned something, though. *There is no end to the week.*
Sunday you can call it but it does not mean
That Sunday anything will end, No indeed.
Time isn't anything. It's rubbing the flat of your fist
Over a wet painting, so time comes on. Then art students
Draw little figures over it in a different medium
So time comes on, the lines imposed
On the earlier smear. I remember Elmer
In his Bathtub Period floated the ground
And put the figures on with it still wet enough to run.
You have to be terribly strong-willed to do that with time.
It's easier to go about it on a dry ground. This is all like
Found Art. VERY INTERESTING is what you say about effects like this.
Within the metaphor so very well might say the psychiatrist
Listening to this imposition of order. Very interesting.
But what are all those gummy greens, what lines disappeared
In the muddied colors, what oh what indeed, I know something else.

You never really find out. A whole new set
Of figures gets set down. You can't go back that far,
You have to find out from the future. In that future
You happen all over without end
And its smear again no line drawings. What would it be
Without line drawings. I can tell you. Terrible.

## *Poem*

How to move you? who sat unmoved
Through the greatest movie ever made, while
We beside you, inches less in stature,
Choked with tears, and on our candy-bar?
                    YOU do not even eat.
Small nourishment finds its way somehow
Inside you from the cold air
and stays there.
                    Crossing the street
Outside the theatre, you did not even
Take our arm. Under the marquee, you had to stoop.

You pass too through walls without echo.
Policeman do not give you a damn.
Doors don't stop you, or halls.
The only question I ever heard you ask
Was for the bathroom, and I remember those replies,
                    So breathless with remorse,
So worried—that it was as if you'd asked them
Something else, as, where their lives had gone,
Into what seedy disrepute or wilful desuetude.
When all you did was wait majestically for the towel!
You never said, *don't trouble*, no, not you.

## *Pique-Dame*

Lady, because they say of you that you are
Bloody and insolent but young and gay,
And that you play better than anyone,
Coming into the game at the end, listen.

Listen, because they say you are unbroken,
That you remained unbroken at the break of hearts, and that
When you look at a diamond, it cracks across. Because
Your court is the last court, standing at
The Threshold of the Great Gates, by the Ice Lakes
Where only the cruellest children, your assassins
Can go skating — hear me.

Pique-Dame, I am losing.
Save me, and I will play you.
I am not played out.
Save me, and I can play.

Pique-Dame, I promise, I promise you,
There will be a great day of leaping,
There will be no unlettered swing!
My jacknife everywhere    no pond no hoop no wheel
Untouched by my red and yellow    my bracelets shall
Roll all over    I on my bicycle will
Cry up the treetoads, what a racket then!
Pique-Dame!
EVERYONE UP    EVERYTHING
VERY LOUD AND BEAUTIFUL    crying red and yellow
Calliope, calliope    every tree breaking
Ponds leaping wild    wheels    trees bracelets birds
The plums are wild    with what is coming
Everything a Wonder    all open hands
Listen!    you've got to listen    PIQUE-DAME! PIQUE-DAME!

## *[You kill me]*

You kill me. Yes you do.
I know no one else who'd
Buy a sparrow (I
Didn't even know they *sold* sparrows)
Just to feed it watermelon
And in public, too.

Every afternoon I think of you
Out there, flushed and fair
Scraping the exhausted rind with a spoon.
Every day! All winter.

## *The Book of Destiny*

(Songs to my Siamese cat – "Destiny" – who eats her young)

1.
Destiny is not eager to claim
Five limber slicker small
Kittens she dropped before New Year's
From an irate womb:

All the doors of the heart have houses,
The greater profiting by the smaller;
The night languishes for the leaner,
While the day waits.

So Destiny is kind to them for a week, for two,
Giving them suck and tongue, but you
Will be angry at what she'll do.

2.
Thick skin in the blow light
Hit a rod with a mallet;
Wholly into the red cave
Flew the marvelous bell;

Light knows something it can't tell:
*Stones see back.*
Hurry, hurry, harries the cat-call;
Prize the temeritous well!

3.
Sic a cat on a dead dog,
Hear the scream of a churchbell,
Hold the night in the eye of a rat,
To snatch the spell.

How high does the day go?
Stretched to the sunrise. Nine
Hours stung in a wasp's tail know,
Heard at a whispering door.

Over the dog's back flees the chill
Hungrily by
The cat's red eye.

4.
The fuss tears the flesh, the terrible tears
Of greeting and breaking are here. Pride strains
At the great howl, light streaks,
And birth cries out at the faces it makes.

When will the winter year, mother, pretender?
Blood is so very dear seldom, if ever.
Pigs into kettles can, light into roses,
But jealousy mangles the suck that it chooses.

5.
Spoil of the night call, sorrow of ever,
Speak to the beast of the petulant morning,
Strike wall of doubt – but where is not ever,
Nor which about, nor benevolence mourning.

Proffer the night spoon, string the white shine;
Destiny, Destiny, never was mine.

You must remember the furtive chill,
The arrogant fruit of the moon, if you will
The noise of the lightning, the shriek of the silk,
The shudder, the shock of the mother's milk.

## *[White of eye, blond of bone]*

White of eye, blond of bone,
The victim always hunts alone:

Yes, I wore this very dress
The night that Virgil died –
And you, as stricken as you were
Remember! I believe you are
What I've been looking for,
And will pretend you were
Not married, nor had a Russian analyst,
Did not eat soup at dinner or refuse
Alcohols, or chew coffee spoons,
Or belch. Such is my faith. For yours:

I only ask you break with me
Almonds; my eyes are limes,
Now yours to squeeze. Or slice
For lemonades. My fingernails
Were not what you observed,
But dames. Not damson plums.
Not dredged with septic stains.
Ladies, ladies' hands. See, lines of pain
Perform upon the potted palms.

## *A Meeting of Several Hands*

A party, a party, we went to a party!
We toasted to hope and the health of our host
In the cup of his porcelain eyes.

*Beauty must be convulsive*, trumpeted our leonine interlocutor;
*A terror we're still unable to bear*, a poet murmured;
*A ripe pear!* said a lady (*in winter*)
She also told us she was going to the Grail. We toasted her.

Crabbed and cold the wine was from the porcelain.
We splashed and sucked—and our generous host turned to laugh at us.
When we shivered and turned to stone, he continued to laugh at us.

## *[Who strained this fuzzy air]*

Who strained this fuzzy air will let me dry
And suck me free of the vines, I shall shiver
Into the landlord heat, drain into the day
And dust into the light at last, free me, free me.

They were leaves that choked me but great leaves
Spanking flat as the broad of a slap
In the world I wanted the Great grew widely
And the Curse couldn't reckon with the fronds
In the world I wanted the Pick and the Claw
Couldn't cut, nor the sad twitch, nor the poor cry,
Where there were no lonely, nor any unhappy

The Curse came in a black storm and the world broke
Everywhere, everywhere suddenly stamping
And all the poor and the rich and the blind and the beggars
Shouting and shaking their sticks; they said,
You are older and have taken your Letter,
Now wear your eyes inside out into your forehead
Else we tear them open like unwanted envelopes, in the mail
You had the crutch, you had the pink stamping horse on the merry-go-round
And the purple sweets, and the drip running out of your tongue
The carnival delights were possible twice at your ticket tips

Now you are done, you are grown, you will take our malice
And believe forever and always there never was anything else.
Sweet we will sweat now, like mountains
Shuddering to grow in the millions of long time
Squashed in the heart of us surely there are footsteps
Of the flying land giants and the walking dragon lords
Hidden in the fern grass, pinched among the silt ledges

All those monsters that kept us alive

# *[Wait]*

Wait.
        Before you take this creature
Who fastened crowding on us like a vine
and call her, RUIN.
                Wait before you say the name.
Signs of love in the changing weather
Signs of love on the mocking billboards
                The beer clock says
LOVE LOVE and could before it could count

Love, love, love still with the proving power
to pull us from our seats  there's a word for you,
still in the language still able to get around

cow's eyes up from the dirt walk, simple spring

        you leaping saracens with bewildered faces
        carrying your keys from place to place, what signifies

        but this

## *[I think I die within the year]*

I think I die within the year, acknowledge
All the chaste formalities of suicide.
You'll go nowhere as you were, and if you did
You'd stand by even water shot with hatred
Having come there yourself the same.
                                                            You have to turn
Become quite simply something other than you were
So looking back to where you were, shall you say
This was not me, is nothing of identity
With what I am, with what I will be
Permit yourself this solstice, permit deliverance
A little death by skinning, stepping free
Taut skin into white skin by, the total anger
Into recommitment, honor it by ritual:
Fast thirty days. On the thirtieth day
Drink only water. Wear only secret clothing.
Speak to no one. Proceed out by moonlight only

*Dear Steve,*

Go south in the winter, immobility
Confounds by the taunt of waste,
but who can afford to go.

Harried,
I remain free. Pressure, principalities
Determine me and I cut shapes, paste them out
Color them and call them by name. Sometimes
They answer, and I seldom lack conversation.

Harried, I am well enough, bend back
The twigs and brambles walking through, leave footprints,
Stamp down a path of sorts. Some follow.
Mostly scratch their own.

Only in silence the crow in the corner
Stares at my performance, makes me make
Mistakes and mix my words

## *[Oh with the sparrows falling and dying]*

Oh with the sparrows falling and dying
And the great birds dipped through the air like moths
Dropped to a flighty death on the sun
The spring to the masked mock world

Sudden, like strangers' white angry faces
Seen and not seen again gone by hurrying
Came in irrelevant darkness and gone again

Lie by the river and mourn her, mourn her
Lie crushed to your side by the dying birds

The morning is refuge, stay in the final stretch
Of the dead sun, stay by the river and stop to see
The masked mock world, stay on for a while for this:
Morning is refuge, mercy, mercy, poor you may be
And crazy and in terror, a little cruel
But here you are helpless, are home, stay there

## *[Rage, but a degenerate rage]*

Rage, but a degenerate rage,
Taking from innocent particulars
Motive, mood, vengeance. A branch that cuts
        A black panther (the fiercest of all the beasts)
        The Dardanelles—I will never go there now.
        Or any of the bargain paradises. Baby, 3 black
        Panthers soiling the plantain leaves at the noon of day

## *[I waited five hundred centuries for the White Crow]*

I waited five hundred centuries for the White Crow
I waited          IT CAME          IT FLEW AWAY
They that told me it would come forebore to tell me
That it could leave me this way,
        More desolate than I ever was
        Isolated out of all proportion
        Moaning, when I am alone, in no language
        Howling like an animal.
        Now on my knees for some reason—
        Clawing my face
I am like this.     If I had known,
I would not have waited. Even listening
To the remembered roar of wings and
The explosions of those first planets which
Screamed going past like eagles
Even still tasting that salt
On my lips my cheeks          Oh Jesus, down my knees
Mumbling your name, mumbling your name

## *[We passed by the irrelevant echo]*

We passed by the irrelevant echo,
The brook ran under the ground and the cavern
And our little bridge that dropped in between

The moss moved beneath us and trickled, the pebbles
Walked with us, from the mountain forests
We called to imagined bears, we were their keepers

Above us the mountains leaned down, so green
And so dark and so heavy we did not dare them
But summoned their shadows, and hid in their depth

All that summer we lived in a cabin
By a white agile brook specked with sun
All summer we pretended we were

Brown and brave, that we ourselves were the summer

Can I know how this was my conscience, how I hang
Now in your arms like a stone, with that to remember
The chaste estimate—as the day before it went under

Remorseless to know we are dissolute
That our limp hands begin nothing, never will begin again
That our legs are too heavy, in their identity

Outweigh that implored dance, our first pattern

Speak: so that I can see your lips move, talk—wisely, purely
I beg you, I beg you, there must be some perfect grace in your hands

## *Fuller Explanation*

This clanking as of old bones
Is fragmentary Patience, fallen off her statue
Dust kissed, chunky, grown up into weeds.

This small violently moving creature, here,
Is myself. This crater of violence
Is a whirlwind, ejected by some deft hand
Into a brilliantly lit space.

This wild and colorful array, here,
Those are my complements. They are:
Anodyne, Opiate, Stimulant, Entertainment.
Bright faces have they, and restless eyes.
Their feet are mad, round and round they move
In unforgettable speed. Betwixt

I stand, balancing
Myself with outstretched arms

In delighted equilibrium.

## *No. 3 CWAC (B) TC*

*Kitchener*

The ice-women live
In an ice world,

Grey bleak, windbreaking,
Hours from nowhere. There the sky
Is a bowl of pudding
And the wind cries across it
Hurrying, chasing, ugly and cold.

The ice-women live hard,
Stare at eachother with rigid eyes
Salute tight lipped
Grimly rise, as grimly go to bed.

## *Things I Have Learned in Canada*

Polish an American white penny with Silvo and you have a dime on any street car.

Save movie stubs if they are pink or tan and you have another ride on any street car.

Quick talking, looking like Jeanne D'Arc, furtive and devious actions will cover up anything you do, if you want to take the bother.

NEVER, NEVER, NEVER reason with a woman. Appeal to her emotions, her ambition and her ego, but never say anything sensible.

Use your ears and you will be able to speak a variety of languages. Speak them and forget your own.

## *The Honey-Bee*

Let us read into the bee
A certain, pertinent morality

(The bee, the bee, which cannot see
Blood red, not that bright stain;

But spectrum spans twice light again,
From sun to sun, and all those dusty violets),
Come let us vitiate the bee:

Pain has a pale face, hold it back;
Bewilder it in pale surprise,
With all the violets our eyes
Reject, why cry a world out into gold,

And strangle pain with pipe note prettily;
Sleep heavily with long gold grasses, oh,
Weep songs to pain of afternoons, sing hymns
To bloodless winds, confound this prison gate with flowers!
Now dazzle this mosaic eye, how generously
With dear infinity of roses! Surely, surely, pain must see
The blushing point, and tremble there
In pastel jealousy. Thus may our bee
Instruct reluctant delicacy;

And eagerly, and pitifully
Protest the natural morality.

## *[Here was the fright, the flight, the brilliant stretch]*

Here was the fright, the flight, the brilliant stretch
Of the dangerous hour; here was the glass and the squall,
The heave of the wheel and the burst of the myriad birds,
Their flap and the shriek they make: But hour, this not an hour,
This was no hour but breathing, no span but a sharp stop,
A sigh's flood, a rib's snap, the flat of a snapped swung door.
Spite the fat glass shattered, the screech of the frozen tree;
We who can speak so seldom only nevertheless always see.

## *The Suicide*

Shocked that she missed the footbridge! She cried out,
But no later than the water she fell in and drowned in;
God help me they tell us she shouted, but she had no sovereign,
No one in the world to tell her to get out of that water.

Now the animals have charted the land for their reasonable holiday,
All have appointed this time to be there to see them;
Photographers capture eachother; the carnival quickens!
The spectres, the hawkers, the talkers, the damned are all there.

## *Subject Properties*

*GEOGRAPHY   Very good. Enthusiastic grasp of geographical facts.*
from my Third Grade Report 1932

Miss Budlong didn't know, but I
Had learned already (to my surprise)
To organize into a feeling order
The monstrosities—I was in love.
My arms ached when I watched him,
At noontime, he was taken
With the others to learn Writing—
We, the girls, learned Manuscript Printing
(Why, I've always wondered, don't
Girls have to write?) and I missed him,
My first generic memory—the unmentionable Garden.
I knew the word for this,
The pain all over, the tension
Watching, the waiting. The firecracker spontaneous
Feelings that pounced and sparked
And that unmindful little boy,
Carefully built, quietly colored,
Graceful—undertaking nothing
He couldn't conquer, like the Writing,
I used to see his arm practicing the curves
Deliberate and unhurried at his desk.
Registered already and on record
The elegance somehow of his resort.
Struck me very strongly,
I tripped and stumbled—
He went his way unhurried
Inhabiting an entirely different world.
There, that is theirs, this mine—

I was hung for explanations,
Nothing hitherto made sense
And here somehow I entered on them,
There is a difference.
What is mine is not yours,
What is yours not necessarily
Theirs. My tears were a relief.
The impossible countries, being
Indicated separate, receded
Into ordered terrains,
Flour and water.
We made relief maps, in the 3rd grade,
That year, I stopped saying the Lord's Prayer
In morning meeting. I waited
For the bolt—it never came.
Having the unanswerable answer,
I asked my mother what proof
She had in God. I got some
Silly answer—(We want to)—I felt sorry for her.
I thought. Up and through 4th grade.
At which time I discovered there were
Others who had thought the same—
That deepened my grasp of distance,
That was almost too much. But James
(his name) by his disinterested existence
Absorbed the phylogenetic consolence.
*I love you so much*. Don't look
When I am looking. Keep your distance.
It explains everything. I love you so much,
We speak out loud and others look.
If we spill—if we splash out—
With love, they are embarrassed.

How could I pray, I had no elbows
How could I look, without knees
Anyway, whose disorderly imprecision
Was this? Did I ask for it?
This trunk, these hands, this face?
Don't do that with your face,
Do you know what could happen, it could freeze
And you'd always look like that. I got sent
Out of class one day. I stood making faces
In the hall. The worst happened. You,
The life center, the focus of all these
Explosive abstractions, came up from downstairs
With a message for Miss Budlong. It was
All right—you smiled discreetly,
Looked the other way and passed along,
It was all right, I learned right then
To be simply embarrassed. Not the all
But only the some. But how do parents
Teach their children that kind of
Pleasant detachment? Europe, January, Mars—
The longest rivers, the highest mountains—
Altitude, Soundings, concomitant lives—
All theirs. I recognised them
But with a growing sense of
Terror and weakness, marvellous James
With nothing on his face but purpose
And sometimes, ownership.
January, Betelgeuse—
Brazil, tundra, stars,
I love you very much,
I recognise my loss
I love you very much,
I love you very much.

## *Hobbes was the most, the end, the wildest*

Economics: We subsist
As Hobbes has taught us,
On things we please
To take from under trees,
Sweet walnuts, grasses,
We shall live on these.
Trigonometry: your face,
Your indescribable lines,
Your hungry bones, your eyes
To fill the hollows
And your hands. Optics:
You know, you see.
Humanities: all that which breathes
By you to me,
Biology and civics:
The quick which trembles,
Our palms, our tongues
All these studies
To teach us how to fill our hungers.

## *[I will give you my wheel]*

A. I will give you my wheel and my skate.
B. Why?
A. I am too excited to say.
B. If you threaten me, I shall leave you.
A. If you threaten me, I shall die.
B. If you are threatened, you should know why.
A. Dying is the last place love can go.
It is its cave, and dark love
Is silent and cuneiform. Your word
Could take me walking to the desert
Because I cannot stand the cold
I could return to that climate which
Is dry and which is under.
B. I will not take your wheel or your skate.
A. How will I talk?
B. How should I know.
Before you learned to,
You could walk, and I who
Taught you to walk as you
Had not walked and how to talk
As you had never talked can ask you
To walk again as you did then
And to implicate no other.
A. My wheel is broken and my skate bent.
B. That is why you offered them.

## *[Then all the listening cries of nature]*

Then all the listening cries of nature cry out Danger:
Sorrow my listening stick, my severage, my savage answer,
Sorrow my text and my animal bruised wonder, sorrow whitely

In the plains where the weather went to walk alone for always
I followed dumb and insolent to all the signs of stature,
Then heard the cries of nature crying Danger, Danger

The world behind me never lost without me, memory
The soft black hang – the birds that broke about me,
Burst from the closet door when last I opened it

The queer cry just distant, the crazed remembered wind,
The terminal scream of the marsh
The net like a bell that swung for us

Now heard against the fading voices, all the sprawl of dark
When animal life vanished, plants dried up and dusted down
Leaving the weather to walk alone and always, walk the stretch of plains

# *American Idealism*

"Keep true to the dream of thy youth"
—Friedrich von Schiller

1.

Sam Lake. You remember Sam.
You swam in Sam and
(*Tears*) drowned. How old were
You, sixteen?
It was white and you
Hadn't liked anything but the Unfinished,
up till then, and the Raven. It's got
to make you cry. Hello, Sam.
See you in the very celibate Sylphides
Of our birthday cake Ides—almost the best.
15 to 25 generally speaking.
The legs of those girls getting across
The third translucent bird measure
Were like salamis, and no one
Should bare their neck like that, after sixty
On the diagonal or anywhere else. Goodby, Sam.
Goodbye rude bridge, good bye youth's
Dream (those Germans were the first to go)
Keep true to the youth of (Schiller)
(After, that is, the Americans. Those Americans.)
Goodbye, goodbye Tchai. & Cie, hello Pre–
Bach and plainsong, salve
Gregorius 2 arms 2 legs 1 wreathing all melodious
Part harmonies library editions on records
Of the history of, goodbye dear Sam.

2.

When we were pistol-happy pop pop all the time
The First Thing was rejection you had to be ridden
Of all riding bang bang Goddamn we could be sorry
For you who had also opera, the last quartets, Don Giovanni
for the wrong reason—we didn't, we knew.
We said so. We carried spears.
Spears, soothsayers, Nones,
We are the blood of the race and its breathing,
We are the chopjaw draftcard bonfires
Through which the adult perpetuates
By which the race endures
We die in our early thirties and bear flowers.

3.

Take a moderate master past his best work,
Reasonably fatuitous: this was a private occasion;
To be asked, you had to have done something,
Or be willing to invest. He wishes to explain
His life by standing axioms, all in his last play,
To introduce his very formal synthesis and in this way
He gets up in front of all of us on Sunday
afternoon in a dark theatre (but for him—they
had the work light on) He makes this gorgeous pitch,
He says *take Cézanne*. They lay all over the farm, in the
Barns stacked against the walls or outdoors lying against
Hedges, what, asked his wife, do you want with them?
Just to *do* them the painter said; here friends, students,
Investors, is your Book of Common Prayer, sear that star upon
Your retina and force your memory or your intelligence
No farther than this and it will not betray you,
Indigent, old, unwell, remember this. They died for you.
NO GODDAMN YOU. That they did not do.
The hot flood burst, the afternoon

Flowed upside down, slammed fist my theater seat, not this
Again not this it breaks the heart, it twists,
It breaks it festers take no heed, the theatre choked and swam—
And calligraphic swans on Chinese silk flowed upside down
Like cranes in carnal disbelief,
Perpetually white became elusive critically irreproachable dancers
And tortured their innocent course as light and indolent
As thieves to take my mother's watch as I asleep and
Powerless lie entangled in the dreams of lost inheritance. Take two.
I lost control, I had to leave the hall.
You cannot, after all, just sit and sob. You cannot *tell*.

## *[. . . the result]*

. . . the result
to write, I DO NOT LOVE YOU, on my heart
and catch it to my sweater like a watch.

## *Love Song (The Rebuff)*

Old crab bit my finger;
Reaching under the rock to touch it
As it should be touched, lingeringly,
It bit me. Wicked secret crab.

*Blossoms burned on the branches,*
*Old birds cried Caw.*

There wasn't a thing on the earth I wanted
But the crab's kiss under the ledge of rock;
I poked my hand in the moon pool
And opened it wide in the dark.

*All for your love dear, all for you.*

Old crab bit my finger. I made show
To the squinting spray and the sea anemone
Of my wound and my wisdom. You, too,
May stew in the juices of the sea.

*Was ever a pretty lovesong*
*Scalded the wicked, sun-living sea?*
*With blossoms burning on the branches,*
*Old birds going Caw.*

## *The Children Will Live with Their Mother (Lyric for the Father of a Girl)*

The child that came a stranger from
A cold, troubled ocean—born
Flushed as a sea robin, wild as a sea lily—

Touched me like morning, and from sleep
I followed her, perplexed, to her dominion,
Marine and violet, which opened like the spreading day.

I tried to lead her into my small, parent precision,
Taking her hand to teach her, taught her names;
Learning at last my language, she told me the hours:

Her feet unlocked doors, windows, hidden ways,
Mines at her touch spilled wide as shells;
Light stung into unlit worlds,

Sand shifted through our listening fingers as we
Walked crab-backwards in the salt sun. I heard.
Seals, just beyond us, barked and glittered.

Surrendering her, I had no longer anywhere to go.
She called me by caught eyes, by my dry tongue.
Having learned me, she could teach no longer,

And we both grew cold by her terror. I told her,
*Sundays I'll come always*, but the sea grew small,
The shore turned black, and the tide flew out in a torrent.

## *Suicide Note*

Before life when I wreathed the wall as a shadow
I loved you all for the entertainment you gave
Your bad and your good alike I loved, I loved,
I was moved by your good and your bad alike.

Now I am older than them and younger than you
And wrapped in life like the package I came in
I can stand on the table and tell you all, all,
All of you listen a moment, to what I can tell,

That I hate you all and I hate you more
Than even my tongue caught now in my head like a clapper can tell
That no more do I wish you but what I've had, I've had
At your hand and your tongue, I wish you may always have that

May this child scream and may that child wail
May your husbands foul and your wives go stale
I wish you no petty dismays, I wish you a lingering curse
I wish that your days all cheat you and your nights do worse.

This goes for all of you, not one left out,
Not one day left unblackened or one night unsoiled
And for the mornings panic then you wake, when you wake
Panic to stare at the celling and look into the morning light

All this I wish you and it is too little for you,
I wish you this, that you always know what is happening to you
That from too much hope you never learn strength
That the world rolls over and over with you and you.

(diminishing returns)

## *[When the light went out at my feet]*

When the light went out at my feet
I flew back, no whale, no antelope
Could ever look at that and start, as I did,
Grey and poor with fright, the night's catch-can

For, not mortal, no where mortal,
No such other flesh can flare
With nerve or borrow fear
From what is neighbor, early by.
Certainly no clothes can cover fur
As we wear, eyes in matted tangles such as theirs
Obscure their thorns, are pink as hornets,
What I try to say:
                    That sallow, naked liver
Thrown up on the beach, was just a warning:
The natural gilly-flowered bear
Ate all but what he left there and went back
To Christmas day without a pang, importunate
And New Years at the corner but
Unfortunately out of sight. Animals!
Flesh and fur, bone and claw,
Picnics of never who cause the grass to grow,
Allow me to watch you. I will be quiet and
Not move the covered ground. I tried all that
Before the light went out, and the tide came in
To tack my legs that were as yellow as a lemon,
                                        and bled them.

## *How to Tell a Diamond from a Burning Baby*

1.

Once he made his mind up, who can tell,
Maybe he was twelve, maybe twenty.
No moaning can catch him now,
No squeaking tree.

A diamond doesn't necessarily look like a diamond
A diamond looks only like a bright stone

All the parts of life are bound with carbon
All the cells of life are carbon bound
A diamond always looks like a diamond
But what we look to see is not a diamond
What we look to see is never there found
What we look for is no simple stone
What we were was light and warm
What we are is cold and frightened
*Everything in nature has an appetite for form*
We would have forgiven you, had you been mortal

2.

The house was on fire, you knew
You knew the difference, too
Between a splinter and a crack
One sure tap
Can even crack a diamond up
The secret is the Point of Cleavage
Baby's burning, look at Baby's burning head
What we are is cold and frightened
What we will be is dead is dead

## *How to Tell a Diamond from a Burning Baby*

Scarlet flavored, drop scarlet,
Catch a kiss under glass

Look through the veined crystal
At the cold embrace

Morning weed, bright scar

Once in a summer dawn
A man left his bed

Left his house
Crept to the wood

Scarlet fevered, spot scarlet

The trees squeaked, a bird called
And the gnats were shrill

The wet grass pulled him
But the grey mist rolled

Morning weed, bright scar

## *[Editors, beat your wings]*

Editors, beat your wings for
Simple descriptions, while we play games.
Or, wish for moral attitudes in
Polished verse, and these
Not harsh but infinitely accomplished.

You do not want our pleasure camps or
Marvellous puns or macabre parodies
Or hipster plays.

                    —I can see you at
Your little luncheons at the Paris Brest or
Aux Steak aux Pommes Frites, polishing
Your glasses on the tablecloth and
Voicing grievances about the class of manuscripts
That, unsolicited, drop down like crumbs
Between the park benches for the birds.

Go, cover your heads with newspapers
In your lunch hours, cover yourselves
Against the damages—and indoors,
Bandage your heads.

# *[It can free us]*

It can free us from the
Tins we are tinned in and the
Jars jarred in and the cans
Canned in

It can free us from every way we are
pickled or salted or dried

The closets locked in and the
Beds we find we cannot move from or
It can make fools of us all        it could tomorrow

You know how it does that. You've seen us
Riding on subways, the love splattered all over
Our honeydew heads and the faces we make
You know, you've looked away when we spoke
We spoke loud and made some others look
We were smiling too eagerly and you were embarrassed

We've stopped you on the street and asked the time
We've started talking to you waiting for a bus
On the subway, it was worse, the others looked

We tripped over your feet in a movie and
Insisted on telling you how we were sorry
That time, we even patted your shoulder and
Picked up your package we knocked to the floor...

You saw us coming at you at a party all smiles
And turned to hide        that was because
You saw us spill the drink and trip on the little table

We struck up conversation with you at the drugstore counter,
Asked if you liked to read...    that time you moved

We looked at you out of a trolley window and burned with love
And you turned frightened and turned in a Fire Alarm,
The Police came, but we had run off, weeping, to play with dogs
We wanted you to speak to us in the street
We were eager to pick up your oranges in the public place
Where you dropped them and they fell all over but you stopped us
Knowing we wanted to make friends

You saw us sitting on the park bench looking hopeful
And happy and foolish and garrulous, and you walked the other way
We heard you say, you can't be safe
We understood—you had seen us talking to ourselves
Or, unawares at that moment, at some game
Like skipping the sidewalk lines, or talking to the pigeons
Or—at our age—carrying a balloon.

You glanced at us making Fools of Ourselves
in the Public Gardens and hurried anxiously on
No one has the right to be hilarious alone
In public you said justly, not even throwing
Bread to the municipal swans and the pigeons that waddled by
We heard your exasperated sigh too late to
Disguise our delight in what we thought was to
Turn into a playmate because, if you looked at us, why
Wouldn't you want to throw them a handful of your own?
We had looked up and laughed and nodded and held out our hands
With the crumbs in them, and our mouths were open to say
*Have some.* You walked through our smiles and left us
To pretend we were smiling at someone else or just
Blink foolishly and try to make friends with the swans.

*Why don't you want us?*
We love you so much,
We could have such happy times.
Or we could just pass the time of day
Sometimes, when you weren't busy

## *[If I lay thinking about the heat]*

If I lay thinking about the heat,
Still pond, cradling the sun,
No one but you would come
Into it, I would turn over
Taking the sun on my skin
Opening and closing my hands,
Still pond, hair damp at the roots on my head,
Listening alone to the underground
Drum sound my heart would make
Into the blanket, sun all damp on my skin,
Caraway seeds on my tongue.

I could be opulent, I knew how,
But now I am poor and the rain comes down
I that was generous when I had so much
Do not look over my
Shoulder now at laughter in the street

The children do what they do and I
What I do, I have no money.
They are crazy to burn what they have,
Their love will not be so much either.

Someday I will stroll outside their tenements,
Rich again, wearing lots of money,
And they will look out with angry eyes.
I will smile slightly. I will have a beachball.
I will never be generous again.
Maybe I will wear a cap I can leave with them
Unassumingly leave it behind sitting on an ash can
But everything considered, *no smiling. No recognition.*
There is too much to lose.

## *Surprise Party*

We are convened to honor a wedding as shall be our annual custom,
Drink it down, drink it down, in the root beer we supplied;
At midnight we shall toast the gallant groom in storebought icecream,
At midnight we shall lick our spoons and kiss the bride.

Then let our arch conviviality fly wild nor spirit sputter,
To preserve the dimpled merriment we swore we'd keep or burst.
Snap the cards and swell the volume, draw the chairs into a cluster,
And we'll spank the lucky bridegroom on the bones across the breast.

The loving little woman twitters, twiddles plates and punches pillows,
Reminds us just one year ago she yielded him her maiden name.
Then in the corner quietly from where he keeps his music,
The bridegroom, wary, waits for us to tell him why we came.

## *Anne, a Chorus Girl Quitting the Line, to Society*

Don't stop loving me when
I leave the Line          next week's routines
Are done with roses and balloons
And one with garlands, all the girls in green
Rehearsing now without me    I will yearn
For large red paper roses that remain the same

Don't stop loving me although
Someone else will please you who
Will do a toe tap to
The Dance of the Hours          Remember I'm
Yours!          I love you better than
A night in costume, or another name

Say that I'm yours!       (I am)
Our Waltz Clog and our Élevées
Were ways like any ways to please
But never face to face          You must
Not love me any longer just because I'm One
Out front (with You) alone       I know

I'm one of You                    I know
That everywhere I'll go
You'll have to know my proper name          I'll sign
I LOVE YOU       and I'll always want you       A*N*N*E

## *Address to the Redcoats*

The Case for the Coonskins. May, 1954.

1.
They didn't ask me to speak.
Who am I, to speak for them?
No one. And by no appointment,
I came, and your faces frighten me,
As always.

But listen.

We can all remember the days
Of the Indian uprisings, massacres,
Rebellions. They are embarrassingly close.
We fought with the Indians, then.
You took some of us captive, brought us
Bread and water, and lectured us.
"Recant." you said, "You'll have
To burn your precious pamphlets.
What's it all worth? Life
Is very short." Then,
Wearing coonskin caps, we spat.

In those days, when we met
To plot against you, and to create
Secret manifestoes for our faith
And defiance—we dared to
Carry no papers. If accosted,
To and from meetings, we pled ignorance
Of even our names, or we stared, silent.
That was before the present age.

Nobody wants to remember these times.
Now we are all at peace.
Everyone likes everyone else.
We are all friends.
Now, we walk the streets as equals.
Electronic chimes
At noon, play themes from
Charles Ives, for everyone.
Little children can read what they please.
We do our work by daylight.

Now, Fellow Americans,
Fellows in *eagerness of heart*,
We have been granted our rights—
You acknowledged yourselves
Gracefully, as always, the losers:
How did it happen, that we, victorious,
Came to belong to the spoils?
What has become of us?
Strangely, we have taken the place
Of the Mercenaries. Whatever
We fought for once, looks foolish
Now. Our limbs are locked in peace.
We are, in grace and fortune,
Non-combatants with good manners.
We tend to forget that you never
Actually trust us—so pleased are we
To have achieved this harmony, this
Mutual respect. No longer roughnecks,
We all wear red coats. As if
To say, although indigenous,
We are civilized.
                    Of the coonskins,
Only a few have kept

Their principles. The rest
Are glad to go outdoors in coats
Of red—or Oxford greys,
Or black ties and homburg hats.
Or academic gowns.
What coonskins do exist
Are murderous, and without honor,
And in low places—
Vestigial reminders of hostilities.
You have assimilated us.
How did it happen? Perhaps,
We were demoralized by peace.

2.
Could it be, you said,
Not long ago,
That what we were about,
Was not a swindle?
In the colleges, you asked,
"Could they be serious?" You asked,
"Might they grow up to be Institutions?"
And in the moment of your indecision,
We moved in.
Moved in, by a slow and considered
Procession, to
The magazines, the newspapers,
The charities, the churches,
To municipal politics, to
The Parent-Teachers' Leagues,
And some of us gladly grew up to be Institutions.
These march in parades,
Campaign for presidents,
Speak at boys' schools, and
Lead Lenten discussion groups.
Or just, from a distance, pronounce.

Moved in we did, we moved—
But when it was all done, and
We could stop, to listen—
We were puzzled by a dreadful silence.
It was all very well when we were proving
How wrong you were about us—
That was the game.
But winning, we wondered what it was,
That we had won. It seems,
You don't know what you want. You never did.

Not first prepared, you usually insist
On nosegays—but we took this
Too seriously, became
Too marvellously accomplished
About nothing. We wrote poetry.
We wrote about summer resorts,
Flowers, and household articles.
Or we achieved this astonishing
And not infrequent *impasse*,
Poems about poems, poems about
Poets being poets writing poems.
You approved, and the nosegays were published.

Even among ourselves, we no longer
Speak too freely. We are wearied, or afraid.
We are not easily provoked.
Controversies alarm us—the last one
Almost set our cause back twenty years!
Years in which we had become accustomed
To pleasant lives, sustained
By generous trustees, years
To peaceably translate the Classics,
Years of hand-outs. Years to let
Our heads grow fat.

Now we turn to look
At one another, and to stare
With eyes like bubbles.
The Code exacts responsibilities.
The New Law says:
"We will accept you, but you must
Supply what courtesy demands, or as
The gentlemen from the Times has said,
Be Wholesome, Positive, and Wise,
It's little enough to ask."
To wit, Society needs, will publicise,
And will subsidize, Yeasayers.

Sometimes, at your bosom,
We've had reason to regret what
We have become, or that we are
Beholden. But,
To bite the gracious hand
That slips into reception-lines
Carrying glasses, on a tray.
Is not for us.
Seen everywhere at work on our Projects,
Fellowships and Foundation Grants,
Or operating our little businesses—
Look at us! We are honest,
Modest, and self-effacing.
Could we bite? Now, I ask you.

But the present choice is ridiculous.
No longer a question of endurance—
The hunger-struck are fed—or martyrdom;
Now, we choose instead
To be priests—or Popular Tories.
The game is done! We've won, we've won,
Take everything. You are not welcome.

3.
You want to believe in Dylan Thomas, as
A Great Romantic, whose life cast
Beams like the sun, go ahead—
We are by cowardice committed
To your displaced applause.
Roethke, you say,
Has taught you what can be got
Out of the garden.
Auden brought you back
To your church, after too long away,
To see a play.
Feed us, clothe us, keep us, pay,
And our way shall be your way.
Together, we'll all honor
Foolishly.
But one warning.

Some, unregenerate, treacherous,
Catty and unvanquished, will be a problem:
Will answer no friendly and well-meaning question
Such as "What are you working on?", such as,
"And when may we expect a volume?", such as,
"And what's the news about your Play?"
With anything but villainous manners,
If not abuse.
Will persist in behaving as if
They were plotting a criminal act,
And you had asked about it.
Will hide away from public inquiry.
Will dread exposure.
Will not contribute to group discussion
Of "What Does Modern Poetry
Mean To Me?" or, "The Poetic Drama
What Is Its Place In This Country?"

Or Symposiums having the theme,
"Are We Communicating?" Will welsh
On social obligations, and much worse:
Will consistently betray their friends;
Will be guilty of sudden, mysterious treacheries;
Will desert their wives, if any, and may not
Support their children. Will even—
As incorruptibles can—corrupt the young,
Who will always want to serve them.
Will say, as Gauguin does, *Life*
*Being what it is, one dreams of revenge.*
And all these monsters will share particulars,
Could be said to *regress*, in the same ways:
That is, they trust no one and nobody,
Certainly not themselves.

They look at all that is close,
And at those who love them, with
Suspicion, save one thing.
Save language alone, and this
They honor and trust, and turn to
In all situations requiring appeal.
If they can be said to be loyal,
It is to language. If honest,
By the honor of thieves, to a few other poets—
And always, to certain powers, which,
In other hands,
Could blow up the Real World.

4.

Listen.
At our house, just as at yours,
They come and deliver the garbage.
It's always been that way,

and probably always will be.
If we adjust—as,
Burn it, bury it, throw it back,
Or into someone else's yard,
We get along all right.

But among the many and singular ways
Of dying, count
The low and terrible strangulation
That happens to the silent.
Among the suicides, count
The gifted children, who could only
Whisper, *You are all fools*. Count
The Silver Swan, who never spoke
Until the end, who leaned
Her breast against the reeds to sing
A single, passionately vindictive song
Before she died.
The day to day hypocrisy, perversity,
Personal terror, private anguish,
Disappointment and loss, qualify
Most of us, But to these
Describing angels,
They are the closest.
Their promised angelism never comes,
And they are all the angrier
For being as they are. And these are
They who come the closest.
They cannot sharc,
And what they do, they do because
They cannot share. And what they are,
They very often hate.

Anyway, look.
Look not unkindly, if you can, to these.
They are only a few, you'll know them—
Bright, convulsive, useless
Or absurd, Because their words
May be the only ones so pitched, that they can reach us
At midnight, awake—or during a long illness.
May be the bird's voice breaking through the dust,
Where we lie lost and sleepless.
May speak for us, when we are speechless.

And may we grant, to them,
Understanding, when
From them, and only them,
We can accept a name
For what we felt, when
It was precious,
Pain or promise
Or fulfillment,
The kiss that no one else
Could name, or keep alive.
—Then, if we honor, honor this,
And if we cannot honor this—
In sorrow, let it pass.

## *The Art of Photographers*

"... is that a thistle is more exciting than a rose."
—Thornton Wilder in conversation

That week photographs flew
All over Nature and landed
Smash side up in the bright blue air

Attention commanded
Everything it saw
Not really real but verisimilar
The way necessity knifes out of all
The lowering domains of imprecision and despair
A word to institute an order—
Well or so we thought
And what we got
Was piercing clean detail.

## *At the Meeting of Two Families*

Who were the assassins that came to get you?
Six of them coated in black and silently smoking—
Slithering quiet like empty clothes

Alert in the dark, from hangers.
Who were they that came to watch you?
Chewing cigarettes they looked at you, they looked at me.

What in a hay moon hovers and waits like a bag
With a man in it? Why did you make
Your face like a Japanese mask of terror?

Limply arranged they waited, just waited.
As always I gave back your terror, I felt it—
I grimaced it, mirrored it—thrust it to you.

And we stared at each other and back to our interlocutors,
The bareback riders from kingdom to kingdom;
You knew them, I knew. You remembered.

Why is your dark like a bag with a man in it?
In the moment of panic, hardly anything happens,
But nothing is true. I remembered, I knew.

I cried out, and the light broke. Your family
Pronounced me charming. My love, my love,
We will scratch all over the earth crawling

The way out of dread we've no name for, cannot tell.
We will come to dread all we own, as well—
Till you wake and weep, till you break the spell.

## *Woman Listening*

Watching him,
Watching his fingers steal around the glass
And the hand tense, and the glass empty again,
And the hand gripping it and curving it back and forth.

Watching the color of the table in the late afternoon sun,
Feeling the sun on the back of her hand and her hair,
Conscious now her hair smooth, sleek, warm to touch.

Looking at last to his face,
Not turned to her but to the sidewalk and to the other tables,
Her glance following his, then back again,
Then falling… to the glass, to his hand, to the shiny table top
        and the wet stain near the glass.
And his voice through all this,
And she hearing nothing that was said.

## *The Recidivists*

My first is to my finger
As my third is to my thumb.

We came in by the fire escape,
But we'll leave by the last room.

We'll take the silver and the bedding.
We're very taking persons.

Be too taken, we'll take too
The hope from your sleeping face.

Frightened          crows
Take fear and run. Their wings

Mudspattered and thin.
Rats run while you can.

We'll take you.    Take two.
Break you, break you, and as we do

We eat ourselves up with appetite.
I hate you, I hate you,

One to the other whispers.
Listen.

You are a liar,
And your cat has no gums.

I do not know the rain from the rats,
Or the rats from my thumb,

But you are a liar,
My first was the first of the world.

## *[My marvelous, my monster squats]*

My marvelous, my monster squats
And ravineous obscures the pass;
Pedestrians crawl through vacant lots,
And motorists abandon cars;

The giant sludge has blocked the crotch—
You can't get sliding by, but you can watch.

He squashes pilgrims in his paws
Especially the infirm or old
Attempt no passage through his claws
And squeezes oozey hopeful bold,
All this, and yet incurious
The lovely pig my monster is.

## *Argument*

Poetry can never be much more than a commentary,
At best, a breathless summation for what words,
What words existed before their source?

Or if you will the eye itself the world it sees
And not the world a body independent of the eye
Then poetry is another world, but however marvelously,

Only a beginning and a later disappointment.
If the word existed before the flood of being,
If the word struggled to become according to a senior plan

Earth, water, intelligence, why then the vision of that order
However faint or obstinately narrow would be all.
But poetry is not word but words, it is not all.

The magic steal relates, subsumes, makes drunken estimates,
Adores, presumes, within a little order; it was never all.
It clings to being with dependent ecstasy; it cannot be alone.

Poetry can never be much more than a commentary. It may be
The quintessential of the race, but such come cheap in nature.
It may achieve the law with accurate economy

Or cry out past the bounds of consciousness, or cleave
The ugly wall, to tear the dark into a further isolation,
Or sop or salvage, or explain, or desecrate, or be, itself, salvation

But this is not enough. It never was enough. Words are not *there*,
Are never absolute to those who love them, do them honor,
Do not themselves create, but feed upon creation, lie upon it

Supplicant as vision to that sum, our subtle force, our sovereign.
Sometime indentured prisoner of fact in space cries out abundant.
In this very knowledge of imprisonment, crying THERE—

## *[Who, if I cried]*

"Who, if I cried
Would hear me, among the angelic orders?"

Forest pavilion of thorns, I walked in,
Murmuring to unseen flowers, staring
At blood on my hands. Alone?
I was always alone, but there were, behind me,
Arrogant footsteps, and before me
Lusterless shadows and partial shapes.

So that I was uncertain, in my speaking,
So that I never knew, in my greeting,
That I spoke to myself with love, or that
My heart was decent, bleeding nakedly
To listening strangers.

## *[With all these justifiable fears]*

With all these justifiable fears that I may cease to be
I'm living upside down in some curious woods
Like needles and mushrooms. Like a grubbing pig
With my nose in the leaves. And to the
Light above the trees, I see it now and then.
You don't want us
Bowed and animal,
All you have
To do is
Make it official.
Say so. Twitch.
We've seen the lightning come and go.
It isn't our fault. Say so.

It's up to You
To do
The Hachacha.
Only You
Can do
The Hachachacha
And only You
Can call the dogs back

## *25 Years*

We got through this year and nobody;
We got through this year and perhaps.
On the day of the white crow somebody
Will kiss us and keep us, but this was not this year;
This year is over and nobody; this year is next year now.

Here is the hole in the wall. Here we peek.
Here is Chanticleer. We shall do everything but speak.
We shall bless, address, abuse—we shall not speak.
Had we to love or were we at fault?
We were confused. Affection and assault
Proved only beasts will eat themselves or anything.
Let us join hands and dance around the naked king!

This year the creeping itch was apparent in the left hand,
This year perhaps it will sneak to the right, we will see.
The eye shivered at the slack it saw it did not understand;
The white crow never came to kiss us under the pear tree.
Twenty-five were pinching parents, poppy-addled, fed on us—
We wept our dusty latter thoughts, we stretched and scrabbled loose.
O! the day of the white crow will come, when it will come it can;
Then shall we shake our sticks, o years, in wicked triumph then.

## *[I have estimated that the value of the glass]*

I have estimated that the value of the glass,
The lovely glass, the broken bits, the memory
Of lucidity only, memory of *size*

Was proper to the evidence of time
Previously lending this house its weight,
Its market absolute, its heavy preference,

Which is to confess to the solicitors
That the house without the glass, the glass
Without the house is a pitiful pass,

We are destitute and invite trespassing.

*A Spirited Chorus for Prudents*

When we tried to climb through the garden wall,
When we tried to climb through the circus tent,
When we tried to take the train (but dared not, after all),
Just at the nick our good sense struck, we never went.
The train, we knew, led out and beyond the earth we knew
By some seven leagues of fright; that stopped us too.

There might have been a happy land. We thought, when peeking,
It burned in wait for us. But now that we are come
To dignity we're reconciled and done with furtive sneaking.
We might have fidgeted as all the silly young have done
In their supposed confinement, and pinched our sleeping
Logs in hot suspicion. O, children yield too soon to weeping.

Surely now we see how we, so young, were wise:
At the circus we might have had to stand and stay,
And stare forever; outside the garden what surmise
Might guess the hour or season, or what strangers had to say.
*And where that train went might have been without return.*
*We might have cried for thirst, or never found the bathroom.*

There now abideth three things, none of which really matter:
The cracked bowl, the sprung lock, the dark of the shattered mirror.
To be sure we cried for each, a tantrum—rebels of cry and clatter,
But now that we're here and appointed they're no realler and no nearer
Then the ghosts of the giddy circus, the garden wall or the train.
If we might and the choice were upon us, we'd gladly do it again.

## *A Sunday Indignity*

While she knelt the boys waited
Watching and sniggering with postures and gestures
Concealed in the hilly humps, down in the grasses.
They rolled their eyes and she prayed and went daft,
And when, rising, she turned to discover them,
They jumped her.

Now consider this embarrassing spectacle:
Around them for miles the river, the silent rise
Of the green, the spiked, disparate wild roses
Grouped limp, with their thorns, and the swollen shrubs
Still in the thick white day, with the stealthy smouldering
Of the hot secret sun;

Here in the heat they were flushed, they were standing,
Her interceptors, proud of their primary life
Indulged in eachother and squat like tubers, undersoil,
Secure in the moist dark, squeezing together.
She was the joke—being caught, being scared—
at the mercy of them.

When she looked at them with terror, they moved
All together, and closed in around her.
She screamed, but the river ran on and along
With the running of the day, the ripple of water rushes,
The upwards cluttered struggle of the growing roses,
The stillness of the secret sun.

## *[Friday I took you my elderly verities]*

Friday I took you my elderly verities
You stood in black shadow with crossed hands

Friday you by a churchyard with crossed hands
And a face I could not see told me a blessing:
I listened but with a glass face.

Over my hands in manuscript were written
My verities, but you did not take my hands:
FEAR was stamped in gold on my tongue, but you did not look;

The bell I brought to sound my signals lay muffled,
The speech I brought to curse you or to flatter made no sound.
You touched silver to my lips, and the verities flattened

Lately, I said, you taught me language. You said,
Speak, and you will not strangle, speak, or you stare alone.
I spoke, and the churchbell jangled

Hour after hour after hour broke upon the town.

## *[I'll write a letter from one to ten]*

I'll write a letter from one to ten,
I'll seal the day with my answer;

You were my joy and you are dead,
Now let the flowers break through.

Pain's populace marched through the streets
In celebration

  dry, dry, wholly by
  why buy fallow when bitter can buy?

## *The Girl Who Wanted to Be a Tree*

She knew to live was to send seed, to root, to live a plant—
He was her rightly prince, her love, in vegetable manner,
The only truly root in all that withered land;
She hoped to flower by her own decay, to swell
And ride to ripeness on the sweep of whole.
Who can be sorry for this desolate dead girl?

## *Incantation to an Age of Stone*

Since you can no longer be
A stranger, you shall be a city;
I shall come,
                    You shall stay,
Incurious in the noon of day
As your great lizards lying sleeping in the sun.

Since I do not hope to learn
A language other than my own,
I shall change.
                    You shall sleep,
And in hot stone your stillness keep;
Then all my other learning will grow far and strange.

You my host shall cast no shadow,
Nor carry hill, not lie with meadow,
Valley or tree.
                    I shall become
Unknown to giant size, and dumb,
Nor season change what I shall sleeping learn to be.

## *From a Fanciful Map in the Children's Room*

The Edwardians were not suspicious
Of symbols, having plenty of their own:
Living (the ones that knew they were Edwardians,
That is) in peace and plenty, content
With their especial pleasures of elegance and
What they called Nonsense, a symbol was
Domestic to them, such as Flag, Tomb, Home,
The Cross. Of sunken and unmentionable symbols
Key, Box, Fish, etcetera, they were innocent,
And innocent they lived, preferring not to notice
Or to recognise what we with childish malice
Found explicit in the iron deer on their lawns.
So they lived and complacently taught Faeries
To children who suspected Nana was a man.
At home we have a map of Faeryland
Peopled by all the adult legends
Found to be charming by the Edwardians.

When you were sensibly inviolate, you could not see
Your mother watching your inconstancy

This country resembles the United States.
"Here they doe magick" is written in one place,
Another, "Here are no soundings", and there were none.
Here men lose their souls, and there they drown.
"Here is Peace Pool." "Here is Gairfowl."

You stretched and broke, the green flood took you out,
You flashed and darted where she could not go,
But piteously calling, tried to follow, follow
Undersea to dumb and show.

At Cape Blanchefleur is shown Leander,
Struggling to get out of the water, and
Shaped like a young girl—Art Nouveau bodies
Were like these, uninterrupted verticals—
The Argonauts shown sailing on Leander, he will drown.
The Snow Queen shown to be innocuous, as she is
Back to, in the water in a rowboat, with no clothes on,
"Here they doe make Snow and Ice,"
"Here is Shiny Wall".

Your light swam wild, her light queered out;
She could no longer see to where you were,
Or longer breathe, or force the waters backward
To call you to her.

Roughly in the latitudes of Texas sails,
On the Enchanted Sea, Tristam of Lyonesse;
He passes the Gold Caverns, by which stand Satyrs.
In this airless afternoon, he does not pass
Solomon's Ship, wherein are Sacred Spindles,
But he is close, too close, to Mermaide' s Rock
"Where they doe singe". The map says this to warn him.
At Georgia Bay, Perseus rescues Andromeda,
Naked, from an ineffectual monster. Near Maine is
The Beach of Pearls. "Here Cousin Cram Childe weepeth",
For what, we never learned.

She cried your names out, joy and her decision,
Who seized the light reflected from your own;
Then when you did not answer she grew shrill, bewildered,
Lost her way and turned to stone.

Where in this map would be Alaska, there are
Pictured steps, and someone on them climbing

Named Amfortas. The Grail is just beyond him.
After that, the indistinguishable tundra
At the top and marked in shadow, then to where
What the children always know is there,
"The End of Nowhere", except that this map
Would place it further from them than the Park.

> Here they doe Magick, here are no soundings:
> Children are not concerned, there is no world but theirs,
> There is not time to mourn for what is taken,
> Or what disappears.

The Park is now a slum, but we are old for parks;
We turned from magic long ago to politics,
Having to learn one's dearest wishes come
By art, by cunning, and by sleight-of-hand.
The house is gone, the Park is done, the boat went down,
But something waits, listens, something always moves.

> Now with all the fathoms measured, time has come
> To call. No one will answer, you will make no sound.

## *Plaint Upon Jack*

He can do just what I do, he can cut off the telephone,
He can cut off the fire and the water and the clocks.

He can be very dull and the colors go out with him.
He can bury little noises. His head can be a fur balloon.

He can lie very still and his swallow folly eyes
Steal into his head and hide hot and sharp and under.

He can even do it dancing. Feet go where
Feet go and eyes go and see nothing, no noise, no one.

## *Hugh and the Pigeons on Fogg Court (Working with Strangers)*

I always know when you're there,
Being able, always, to hear
You up on the glass roof, scratching:

I can hear your claws and now
And then your cackling coos; sometimes
You turn around, and, looking downwards,
See me looking up and watching
All the way. But usually

Attend your own, emboldened
Though you be sometimes
To fly down suddenly. To settle by
Some statue's quiet, heavy arm, therefrom
To stare incuriously.

                                        The whole court anxiously
Performs upon your trespass,
Which takes from you its sounds. The light
Which glances from these serviced stones
Reflects to you, and answers to your names:

The echo overlooks the onlookers,
Which hears, and bells, and honors
Your disinterested nearness.

## *Anyone looking at you sees—*

You stand away as clear and careful as twelve trees
Against the Arctic circle, as
Near as could be green, and
Not far from the Arctic sea.

Your hands have shadows
Of leaves, into the palms,
Your fingers over these
Fold, to make a fist
To keep the shadows fresh.

As if you stood in summer in
Finland, you do:
And others slept all night by sunlight
But you, who turned to
The ocean when at midnight
The dusk fell,
And there was no one else
Awake, to see the Arctic Circle
Or the white stars.

## *[As* commedia *players]*

As *commedia* players
We cannot fool the City or ourselves,
Too tense, we soon go shrill,
Lines painted bright go
Gray, in the hot lights,
Reveal the twitch and pull.
We will never be Favorites.
We had best go on by ourselves.

You were very dear.
You were very close to me, even in your anger.
However we are, thin or poor,
I will know where you are. Write me.
Tell me what you are playing.
I will never again nag or break up.
Write me and tell me where you are.
—I'll always answer.

## *But You Can Fool the Camera*

When will you be at home? When can you learn
The improving light that lights alone?

                                        The sun
Is *vieux jou*.
Knows only how to
                                        Kill and keep, and run machines
Let it be, let it go
There's room for you here too
                                        Here in the dusty frissons
                                        Of the sugary poplars and aspens
                                        Out of the noise of the seasons
Tell me why
When I sat with my hypocrite pale brothers
You passed by
Pretending not to see.
                                        Come here under the tree.
We saw *you*.
                                        There's room for you here too.

## *Old Belle*

I did not live by the land, I did not watch the sky;
I took one rich harvest after another from the sea.
One day I saw the nets were thin and wondered.
The next I was frightened and bought new equipment.
After that I was frenzied and my savings went fast.
I am not bankrupt yet. You can taste time in my gestures.
While there are drugs and liquids and solids and solvents
Manufactured to daze and to shield and to mask
Loss and panic I shall have them. And each time,
Still, that I make loud my original investment
My competitors, grown old as I am stiffen and look anxious,
Buried in their rooms with the ruined photographs.
What I cannot understand is the injustice: I, as
Few can boast, worked ceaselessly and sacrificially
Sparing no yearnings to talk, just for once, greedily
About myself or to laugh out loud in my partner's face;
I knew the rules and I obeyed them, even despising them,
With exquisite precision. Was it for this
The craters opened up and sucked the springs inside?
Is it just, I ask you, when I worked so desperately hard?

## *[excuses, excuses]*

excuses, excuses
shrimp pink and rotten veal
where my cadaver
lies sleeping
          lily or
carnivore
lie down here weeping
pale teeth around the ring
crowds
wonder
make no reprisals

## *Dummy in the Crowd*

We, amiables, thumpers, animals—
Tumblers and performers of a very little fate—
Might have forgiven him (for all he did was stare at us!)
Had he but acknowledged us, sadly, his complicity;
We only asked he *suffer* that complicity.

We were his family, and wept for disavowal;
He stood outside the ring in proud disguise, he masked
As audience. He might at least have clapped his hands,
Applauding us, acclaimed our dance in bottle green!
But he who danced for no one clapped his hands at nothing—
Oh, by his scorn of us he orphaned us to shame!
The children grew distorted in his glance, the women plain,
And all of our pleasant antics seemed ridiculous;
Even our marching animals seemed ridiculous.

There were those of us who hated him, and disappointed children,
And we did not forgive him, who betrayed us by denial,
Whose mockery was immobility throughout our Grand Performance;
But had we seen our child take aim we surely should have stopped him,
Who severed murdered head from neck by sprung cork of a pop-gun.
Oh when we knew, we flew, we flew to him with pity in our eyes,
To find he was not real at all, but bound to joint with wires!
He was our blood, how could we know he was a dummy?
No blood of ours before has been a dummy!

We bade him rest, and stood about in strong variety,
Sad in our bright parade of pantaloons, of coloured hose—
And all of the leaning curious, the paint concealing
The wonder on our faces, bent to look at him.
Then, where there would have been (from children) laughter,
The elders of us scolded us severely, saying:
*Let his assassin weep for him, let melancholy women*
*Fold on his sawdust heart his hands, by his paper sword.*

## *[Where lovers lay around like great horned owls]*

Where lovers lay around like great horned owls
Shot down that day, the flying feathers
Shut away the sun—(someone has said
If all the birds fell from the sky at once
The whole earth would be blackened for a day—
But these were only the larger owls.)

Lovers. They lay
Exposed, their bare legs broken,
That kicked, and looked like broken twigs
On subway steps, in alleys,
Doors, on all the poorer avenues
Lay with itinerants like them,
But dead, not sleeping

No one shot them down, they that lay there
Had turned upon eachother in the air—angry.
Everywhere, feathers fell, but in the night before
Like city soot and cinders, no one not loving, sleeping,
Saw them or recognised the dying fall or saw
The flying bodies hit the street

## *Death of Another Swan — Miami 1953*

To die out of debt was a last stand, but
Somewhere the outpost of a father in Tucson
Blind, angry, married to his kitchen radio
And the gossipy neighbors who would have caught the post

Some meddler would have come into her room
Discovered the awful secret and written
The meddling letter, she had a panicked vision
Of animals beating about the nettles and weeds
Snarling and howling just outside the wire enclosure
In Florida the weeds are full of snakes
But she was never any further from the cold mountains
Or her birth on an Illinois farm than a dead sleep
After losing at the races, or after losing a man
Who could have been good to her, if she had waited

Muddied at noon at the hotel bar alone
She did not live there, she came to hear
The noise at lunchtime in the cabanas nearby
Looking at the bar telephone as is, she having
Left messages at her rooming house it would ring for her
At any minute and say *Come*, I will give you everything
Now that you asked everything that I refused
She stared blowsy focus at the collection agencies
And the finance company and the pink convertibles
That cruise Collins from dawn to dawn with salvation in them
Wearing tropical shirts and the smiles of the victorious
Always ready to stop at the red light and say
Going my way? Hello beautiful. Or just Get In,
To glimpse salvation over the inevitable discussion
Of means, or is it ways or the simplest statement
Of kinds of pleasures

The trembling vision of

Angel's faces red rimmed, turning to snouts,
Eyes pin pointing and the cheeks swollen out
Or one scream in the dark in a boarding house bed
Having woken altar from dreaming of a pig's back side
Where the smiling cashier had been stripping
For action, his hands trembling, his eyes
Bright with love

She told the bartender, I've been sick,
And slipped from her stool from her stalk
Like a cracked stem when the wind is blowing
And the monster bloom was not staked
He knew her: "You've been borrowing money."
She was ready to steal, but not clever
Like the others and he stared at her sadly
She looked so pretty that day, they all laughed
When she picked herself off the floor and dazzled
At them giggling with the happy fatuity and absence of blame
One goes into bars to find, the peace, the concord

An arm sized her brown hard forty year old skin
And helped her *Smiley, what for you grease the seats here?*
You are among friends, the dizzied room said,
A glass stem fresh and cool came down the bar from her,
The gentleman at the end would like the blonde to join him

The wind trembled with lilies and jasmine
Some sound water running bright and cold nearby in the ladies room
She shuddered with the effort but tied around her
The mink stole that was her beautiful affirmation
The tropical plants leaned to her in their stands
Buried in lavender free forms from their places
Cut out by the decorator in the beige wall to wall carpet
And she heard them, tender more tender than the palms
Which hiss and breathe at night like users of narcotics who are sleeping

## *Death of Another Swan — Miami*

*("Mon Dieu! Quel catastrophe!*
*Il me devait quatre francs.")*

Savage now with hunger at midwinter
Still grasping at the plunder of the swifter
She begged in order to be able to steal

Fruits and flowers and crawling vines,
Snakeskin envelopes for her arms,
Bird feathers over her face

And a sack to cover her, all of her,
Up to her neck where the dry plucked skin
Peered out, tied about with a bow.

Sitting so, she unlocked her throat,
And spitting her last, defied her creditors:

"When I die, leaving loneliness triumphant on this earth,
When I die as the impoverished sun snuffs out in a bag
When I die let them tell all the world what I know:

That the wise are devoured by fools with red eyes
Now let wild pigs claim the rest of you"

# *Who Is the Real Oscar Mole?*

Lodged under layers of things in his mouth
Are words we haven't heard since Editions
Minuit (peuples! à genoux!) cost us a
Sou or two but oh, the times our money had:

His nom-de-plume has a funny beard and a
Violet cigar. He is *always* where we are.
From the sidewalk, he sees us, and stealthily,
Before we can cry, WAITER! he reaches for

Our glass of Byrrh, or, turning up his nose at it,
Your glass of "Pschttt!" or your *Perrier-citron*,
Then he bubbles at the waiter and offers him some.
Who is he, really? His nose holes quiver with derision.

O, he has a wildebeest's eyes, not nice,
And a tongue like an ice pick, he could core an apple with it,
But he speaks to movie stars, and rides to parties in their cars
With them to take part in violations—

Or where, at the very least, an important new
Perfume is introduced. Oh introductions!
We think, if he would give us any, or a few,
We could at last do all the things we've wanted to,

Some day, we think, he must.
But now he doesn't want to see the pictures in our wallets.

You know that Poison Tree of Blake's? well look at ours:
First a plantain, now a palm, until we sit in darkness
Under giant fronds which Oscar susurrates,
He knows he makes us cross and jealous. Yes,

But where is the monkey in the tree to throw the nut
At Oscar's head? There isn't one because,
If Oscar Mole is real, there can be no real monkeys.
Horror! it is our money, but he has ordered a *fine.*

## *Lines for Mrs. C.*

*—about to annihilate, in a long succession of cat murders, two old stray cats with ether, in her washing machine, with the cover on.*

O you cats, go home to God,
Kitties, where the saints have trod,
You go, you two, you too
Like thin flames upwards into
That which, electric and ethereal,
Is going to be your first square deal.

*She finds them and locks them in the kitchen.*

Kitties, go! Unspring those tails!
Cease wild scrabbling of those claws!
No longer roll these maddened eyes!
—Trust me,
kitties!
I who love cats know their problems.
Tonight you will sleep in the arms of
Jesus.

*They are not convinced.*

*She puts the cover on, and sighs.*

They say down here you never knew
What life could be, because we stuffed
you
Into the emptiness of ours.
—Well, yes.
But life is vile. So are its pleasures.
They say, you animals that came in with
us
Never had a chance. Horsefeathers.
Life is vile. So are its pleasures.

*The struggling grows fainter, and she waits.*

Mortal love was not for us and neither was
The Cross. We chose you.
Oh you cats, take from us
Our emptiness and our loss.
We have to lose you.
Go kitties, go, go home.
Kitties go home, go home.

*She looks, and is satisfied.*

## *Love and the Social Worker*

The voluntaries of the city
Tried to explain to him
How pity was an indignity
He hugged to keep him warm.

He permitted them as he had been
Rude to them, although he came
To march in the candlelight stamping
With all of them.

*Break*, they told him, *and spill,*
*Everything will come*;
But he broke from them at a window-sill
And climbed home.

I shall hide, he said, and they
May march and storm.
I will not look again nor will I buy,
Nor will I turn.

## *[Drum eat drum]*

Drum eat drum, river beat river,
The symphony is under the water
It was on Tour    nor the men are all drowning
They all went intogether look at what is floating
Tearing up the white froth    forty folding chairs
Stand and stare and roar above the water
The falls are behind us and the cliffs below
Birds shriek and even the animals left long ago
Drum eat drum    there were two of them    they are fighting
The white one will eat up the black one, but
The black was kinder, wanted to love, killed no other
But himself    it was his own flesh he cut open, causing
The white one to lose his temper and to strike him
The black one was paid less than the white one, why did
He strike him, he had no name
            Forest eat forest    tide come night come
Cats come to look around when the storm is all done
Cats come to stare and lick their feet and lie down
And yawn all over the mountain where it happened
The Conductor, he perished, he opened his mouth and
The water went down him like thunder, made him heavy
Filled his pockets and swelled up his breast, he drowned
Before even the company could warn him    cats could not care
Pines will grow tall where it happened
And all the recording equipment the cables like congers
The base metals the huge boxes gone, gone, gone

## *From the Car*

(Signs on highways in Massachusetts, painted flat figures of children, say *Drive Carefully—School Children*)

The wood was filled with painted men,
Lost from their postures in some suburban garden,
Under the bird house, over the bird bath,
Out of the light and the sound of the highway.

The road lay apace with the hill. We had just time
To get where we were going (if we knew). We went.
There was a signpost, painted red and blue, ahead.

"There's a child in the road. Don't miss."
"A child? There is no longer any difference."
"No longer any child but this?"

We did not look back. We did not trespass
Irresolution had chanced here and lost—
The choice had passed. We knew our own indignities.

The trees were painted red and blue; the wooden men
Continued in their pantomime. The wash and pull
Of light crept in, restored the dusty highway.

## *[I've come a long way for your sake]*

I've come a long way for your sake, since
You held me in two to keep me from
Breaking, perhaps, in your arms.

Then my back was a bone by itself and it
Cried in the dark like a dummy alone,
All wet with cologne and tears

You struck to stay like a nail too small
For a mirror that hangs on a plaster wall
And crumbled as it would, but no glass fell,

And no wrath shattered our pitiful silence,
Oh, in emptiness such as this, the wonder is
That pity is so vast, and touches! These dark objects

Came together in the room, and dried by morning,
The fan shut off and the dummy wakened
To stretch its neck in the dry hot air—

## *[Cats walked the walls]*

1.

Cats walked the walls and gleamed at us:
You remember, I remember,
The ceremony at ache's place.

Love you, love you I do, love you,
Ham, shank and shoulder, lights too.
You remember. I do.

2.

The dead planted the holly, it grew like hair.
The dead sat back and sucked their crooked fingernails
When you and I set out with our haversacks.

The road had a million suggestions;
In return, we kept irritatingly silent.
Finally annoyed, we jumped out of our skins.

We stripped our hair and nails, and stamped
Upon the road, which kept it down. After that
We blew up like balloons and blew along.

The air astonished us by heaving. We flew,
We grew quite wild, our faces turned to smoke,
Our eyes peeked through. Like pebbles under snow.

All this some time ago, and only our bones remained
To answer bells, to say hellos.
To ask gay questions in ski clothes, after dark.

3.

On a mountain in the winter, a little mountain,
God knows what you'll find. Christmas trees. Bright
Little berries. White animals that smell and flee.

Birds in an icicle tree. And underneath the snow
The minerals burn black, and blood, and nervous blue
And diamond and mine. The bushes creeping through

Cover them over by boney fronds. They creek and stir.
The animals do not care. The wind falls down.
No one minds. The birds fly furiously back.

4.

Now about the dead. They cursed us.
Just at the time we climbed the bend, they cursed.
We came upon them in autumn, bent to their mineral planting.

We waved to them in Tyrolean caps. Halloo!
It was they, we discovered, who had to
Plant all the mines, and mulch them.

Everything but the animals, who were
Elsewhere planting. We're here to help you!
We carolled, which is when they turned and spat.

I have a cat who walks walls, and watches us,
I can guess who planted *him*. No mordant wrong
Has been righted since that time. No fine thing

Has happened or been said, no dead or living animal,
No mineral, no winter-growing vegetable
Has laid its hand upon our hearts or touched us.

We are pale enough. But that's not good enough for them.
They listen eagerly. They hope to hear us coughing.
You remember. I remember. Here they come! Hurrying.

Love you, love you I do! Love you!
Ham shank and shoulder, lights too,
All their child faces are lit up with laughter.

Today they clap their snow hands. White day.
The woods are filled with them, and the mountain trembles.
Below on the plains and the marshes, the mirrors shiver.

And the numb sky rattles like a dim old eye
Straining to see in a giant gourd.
Nobody shakes but the living, and they can see.

I remember, you remember. Love you.
Love you I do I will I do.
Ham shank and shoulder, lights too.
Brain and liver. Love you.

## *Obstacles, Loyalties, Deceits*

*For Hugh Amory*

I have never understood how someone
Who is one of the first in the world should be
Told what is so by one of the least of the world,
Who is not of his family.
                                        But so it goes on,
That these stars, which burn their lives as suns,
Are continually directed on
Their courses by their satellites. These
Are willingly pushed, the power is trust.

I speak of the good fanatics, who anger us,
But who push our world to its frontiers;
These—why is it?—are as loyal as this
To their betrayers, or to even
One of them: clever, he is, presumptuous,
Opinionated, proud, and always, passionately,
More articulate than his betters.
                                        One—what is his secret?—
Who whispers lies to proper genius, which
Should only listen to itself; one
Whose weight commands him like a stone
Which buries argument, which weighs him down,
Which drags him where he could not go alone.
Behind the First I often hear the whispers
Of these bewildering charlatans.

## *George and the Different Kinds of Light*

Nobody noticed but George, that
The light in the kitchen was hot and white,
The light in the room was yellow and warm
The light elsewhere was night. George
Was gentle as he was wrong. All that he did
Gave him pain, but he laughed at it.

Such laughter was very sad. We loved George.
George loved light, but never understood it, quite.
We understood neither George nor the light,
Nor looked too long for the light,
But George we agreed on; we loved George.

in the castle of the lost echo the poetic equipment
rests under sheets in the dark. Spiders over it
scrabble to cells in the gullied windows, sound nor light
interrupts the vision of the moth or the damp bat.
The swan we knew clings to its wooden wings in a grace
all of itself, with a sheet on its neck around.
Melodious properties lie unrequited and forlorn
whose string and pipes are outworn, now in order
too well played and certain to be useful, sorry toys
of pure incautious noises never played. We put away

everything we learned to play after the lesson.
We learned well and here it piled up, order on order
And the swan came at last to the bat, the dove and the gull
Squat together because we knew them too well. The lute
went first and lies at the bottom of the pile…

from the cold shoulder to the grave
from the impolite cave we remembered to caring
we leaned on the props we insisted
were useful.

## *[This day came up as a fat squall]*

This day came up as a fat squall,
Dangerous and black, with a swollen scowl:
The winds tore into the beach, the sand
Puckered and tore, the waves were rent
With wildness and hightide anger…

… By general consent
Like allowance. Thursday shall be
The maid's day out and Sunday we
Shall permit a pinched sobriety
Proper to our status and position to abate
And trickle from our faces smooth as oil from slate
And all week long we learn to mark inchastity
As healthy thinking…

Lovers, lovers in the wood
Hugged eachother as lovers should
Lest the world should crack,
And the world should turn,
And the lovely break, as lovers learn.

## *[Hard stamping wind]*

Hard stamping wind, queer crazed wind:
March I know like a bad friend
The long boredom, the mutual weary expense

Know it and keep my white eyes
                                        but March is truer

The joy, the riot, the silly expanses
Never last very long, after that it's a matter
Of trial and attention, of letting the hands go slack
When they shudder to grab or to strike:
Wherever you are, whatever you are, it's an effort
To know that and for always

## *[Doctors, lilies of the plain]*

Doctors, lilies of the plain,
I resign my long attrition
Dears these dollars are all yours
And all these flowers
Flowers small and flowers tall
For Dr Os and Dr Sybyl
Pink Chrysanthemums and purple
For Dr Ur and Dr Organic

## *[Came up the long stairs after a long time into the dark]*

Came up the long stairs after a long time into the dark
the highways still going under my feet over my head
under the underpasses up the valleys and into the hills
to feel your bodies racing overhead scaring the dark like
you used to, violent and graceful, grey and spectral
I remember you, I remember you, you were so fair and inviolate
You had red eyes that rose out of the black rug and stared
You climbed curtains, at any time you could be clinging up there
at the window, bodies shaking and heads set to the side looking down
claws clutching their hold
cats all over the back stairs    if I reached out
I might have touched you    you would indicate
some little passion about having me back, strike
sexual attitudes and writhe, or scratch and shriek,
I remember your conventions. They meant, now we eat,
Or we were very beautiful and you were not there,
When that act was over you would go limp into silver lines
And beat your eyes down again to blue, and leap on
My bed by the time I had put my suitcase down
And lay there just before you    you who
would take my feet like animals you knew were harmless
and stretch there licking in the warmth    I loved you
You were solitary and brilliant and coocoo    we made
continual demands on eachother, and when defied, got mad
each to each and cried loud and mad or scratched, or
I kicked you but our lives went on nevertheless    wild and devoted
and to eachother nameless and you were always there. I fed you,
You came to accept me. You paid no attention to me when you went mad
as you did    sometimes after eating    or sometimes just hungered
leaping to twenty times your length or screeching
or racing up and down the room and the hall and yelling in the stairwell

## *To Frank's Guardian Angel*
## *(To the Guardian Angel of an Aesthete Going to the Middle West to College)*

May he, secure
In peacock fur
And Manner
Go in your favor,
May he wear
One crocodile tear
Stitched to the cheek at
The corner of the lid

*You pray for him, you weep instead,*
*Keep his appointments, bless his apartment*

Protect him from
Violation:
Bogs not creep,
Bugs not come,
Burrs not crawl
Crows fly white,
Caves not cackle not beckon;
Let him keep his Three Noses

*Save him from the malevolent eyes of*
*Spiders but neither throw him to the swans*

And shine on his spotted tail!
Yes on his spotted tail,
Respect his reason,
Protect his tongue

*And in the jasmine and buttercup*
*Season of parricide, flower him*

## *[At last the Indians have their summer]*

At last the Indians have their summer.
While the rest of us were at the beach
They were waiting.

## *Born Old*

1.

The house was on fire, he knew:
He woke before dawn and still

As the upstairs breathing he dressed
And dropped from a window sill

And edged to the wall of the garden,
And crept unseen to the hill.

2.

The woods were as hushed and as dark
As his sleep, but he found his way,

The forest squeaked and a bird
Cried out, but he pushed them by,

And the wet grass plucked at his knees,
But he scrambled through to the valley.

3.

He looked back once, and saw
Where the ridge behind him was high

The lion his love, grown little,
Stand anxious against the sky,

But the house was on fire, he knew
And he blundered through to the valley.

4.

The valley was flat as glass,
The sun was hot on his head

Soon, he lay down on his back,
And slept where he struck his head,

And he shook with the spider's twitch,
And stretched in a caked web

And woke in the dark for the lion who
Once struggled into his bed.

## *A Child's Fantasy*

When, early ago,
Stalks rose over my head and the line
Of the land escaped my eye, I

Telling myself nasty stories in bed
To amuse myself on the longest night of the year
Wound my early play green fingers around my head
And tied to the brass bed posts my braids.

You beckoned from the near wood, a crow call,
I heard, and jumped out of bed, and crawled
Down the trellis, delighted.
Not to tear my nightdress, I came
By the low fence. Not to wake the sleeping dogs.

One dog woke and followed after, you were cross:
"Whose dog is this?"
I said, "My family's, of course."
"Will he go home?"
"He might not, he's dumb."
"He should not have come."
He followed us to water, then we turned on him.
We tied his head up tight with muslin,
We weighted him with rocks we found,
And giggling, pushed him in, and stood and watched him,
And poked him down with sticks until he drowned.
"There's for *him*. He won't tell now."

"Let's swim."
"They'll hear us."
"Who cares." We went in.

The moon spilled all over and trees walked on the river.
I screamed.
Stories I told out loud came alive on the wall.
Faces crawled out of my hands,
Slobbered and winked and crawled
Into every place.

I called
*No* when the dog barked. It banged
All over the house and the doors slammed.
The dog walked into my room and stared.
The dog walked into my room and stood.
Everyone came angry.
The dog isn't dead.
I know *I know.* I was just thinking.
In the window to my room my twin looked in,
Winking. Go to sleep again.
Winking. Play dead. Don't tell.

## *[Now you will make penance]*

Now you will make penance in the best way that you know
For the bowels that ripped wide out and bled, for your loose hands
For your face that could not hold together but swing down
And your lips that fell weakly

For the sound of your hoarse voice when it sprang out like a beast
Out of the way of your control, for your knees that crumbled
And your hanging arms, the eyes that rolled
Crazily in their sockets, all incontinence of joint

> Move in the cold gray rain, speak clearly,
> Chance the word at the lip, remember the articles;
> Only the dance is chaste, to absolve those late loose hands
> And the heavy trembling limbs you must make them serve you
> In the fine stretch of form – then as you go walking
> Into the memory dance, all your limbs perfect, timed
> By your voice and your eyes straight ahead of you

Burn out your decomposure, tighten, tighten,
Burn back your way to grace, only grace can absolve you

## *[When I came back up out of the dark]*

When I came back up out of the dark (Tuesday)
With the dark still on me, a kind of you
Stared me down like a dead sun

(And I in my black crawl wondered,
Knowing where worms were, mud and spoil
And silence, what should I owe a dead sun)

But shriveled coming up, and that was my delivery,
And shed as I walked upright all my reasons,
Ash and a little lost frenzy. Pity me.

Pity the skin that tears and the skin that leaks,
The features that hang loose, the inert limbs,
The hands that cannot clutch, that cannot speak,

Pity the breakage, somewhere leaked away the core
And the skin with the tear cannot cover,
Pity the healing fluids spilt upon the light,

Pity the flowers broken at the stem, pity the crack
And the shattered and the torn, pity me not them,
We who break them, we attend with fright

Our damages, too late, we learn them,
Then go underground, go home escaping them.

## *[Went down a warren of his own]*

Went down a warren of his own
Went to a warren down, down, down,
Through fears and small scratching sounds
Gasping as he slipped just past recall

Why did I lose my third best? What was
The melancholy curse that came to and
Clung to us without reason? But despite
Wronged streetcorners, vile opinions, and feelings
Between us that thronged all the public stations
Like ancient obituaries, I still wore
My first best for this: my extraordinary sentiments
Were called into use—and hesitantly
Considered intimacies into death

Nor were hat and shoes not part of this,
We could have made of them anything we tried,
Sunday or East Wind, a boat trip, a processional.

## *A Jingle for a Man Who Held My Hand*

Lay satirist and self psychologist, wear
This pretty friendship until maggots tear
Out both your eyes, in slimy insolence,
To make a mockery of our impatience.
Hold my hand, patronizingly, in yours
Till fingers folded forming claws
Dust to memory of bone, then sigh,
   Then mark this presupposed affinity.

Now our like minds are folded into each.
Embarrassed loyalties found speech
In silent recognition, speech in scars
Where we lay jeering at the tinsel stars.

## *[I can't do anything for George]*

I can't do anything for George, he
Won't let me, I want to, when my eye
Was red as a cut star he took it out
When the wind blew it far back up
57th Street we laughed, my tears fell away
That was after he broke my foot

Like the stem of a glass and bound it dry,
I kicked the other foot wickedly,
But he didn't frown, he just went away
With his tenor aria and his beret
Now I have nothing any longer that bleeds
Or cares, nothing to do with my hands—oh
Now what can I do for George?

All the horses neighing, *George*, children
Playing, saying, *George*, Policemen,
Smile at him. You, junk collectors,
Milk deliverers, burglars and bums,
Smile at him.

You, days, dogs, carpet layers—
Do as he says.

(But I'd wear my clown's suit for him
Anytime he wants me to, or show him
The Haunted Room, or sing him
The Rowdy Song.
Anytime he wants to
He shall be led to the Diversion
or the Cranny. Anytime he says

He shall have my pillow slip to put
Over his head. He shall cut eyes out
If he wants to. He can look through
                    At the room, at the Cranny
At the jumping spiders, at Selected Shells, at the Wart,
He shall eat my peach, if he wants it.
At anything, and I shall sing the Rowdy Song.)

All the horses neighing, *George*, children
Playing, saying, *George*, Policemen—
Smile at him! You, junk collectors,
Milk deliverers, burglars and bums,
Smile at him.

You, days, dogs, carpet layers,
Do as he says.

## *To Our Friend Who Married a Bore and Who Is No Longer One of Us by Choice*

Not altogether generous, we watch you go,
Complacent, to the sun and air
And take your time to get there.

With backward look you frown at our still argumentative
Faces still propped open wide for discourse,
Surrounded by the fact of your decision.

You leave us speechless without matter to reply.
All *we* can hope till sundown when the waxworks die,
Is that you trip in journey, hope you do.

Perhaps your baggage breaks and springs wide open,
Scatters at an unsprung lock, embarrasses you—
The detail left undone at parting.

All we can hope, with still, malicious waiting
Is that *you will need us then*. That you will search
The lonely sun and air for our uncompromising faces,

Beg bored trees for our forgotten arguments,
Scratch the air and try to find a listener
Where they never any longer speak our language.

Oh yes, when you will feel more fondly of us,
Depressing as you are, and you will be,
Think that you left us cosy in the climate of chagrin.

Perhaps you'll even miss us.

## *Children at the Zoo*

Where are the bears?
Where are the seals?
                First for the bears:
                We'll find their dens
                If we follow the signs.
                One, rough and golden,
                Will bow and dance.
The bears were no good,
Where are the seals?
                Take my hands,
                If we follow the signs,
                We'll know them by their shining skins.
                We'll applaud and they will bark for us.
The seals were no good,
Are there some elephants?
                He didn't want
                The peanut, he trumpeted,
                The dust blew up
                And settled on his dusty back.
                They stood and looked
                Older than God,
                Sad, in their big skins.
We hated the elephants,
Where are the lions?
                Take my hands,
                Close your eyes,
                We won't be frightened.
Are these the lions?
                Yes.
Is this all there is?

There are the tigers—
Asleep like the lions,
Look at the tigers.
The monkeys were no good,
We hated the birds.
Buy us an orange drink,
You promised.
Keep hold of my hands.

## *[What should I do in Illyria?]*

What should I do in Illyria?
That is the question.
No matter with what charming tint of violet
The smoke from yonder peasant's thatch arises
Down in the misty valley
Such charm holds no surprises
For one who has lost, is losing touch
Lost, and is losing much
In the misty valley.
What should I see?

The monuments and palaces of interest
That do renown this city
The campanile in mid-town Manhattan
The Lexington Avenue friary
And the palm tree
Blooming forever, madly, at the Plaza
(Martinis and silk-sheathed knees in that bee-loud glade)
Offer no shade
To the dusty, hot, be it said
Sweaty traveler.

True, there is still a charm
A mystic longing
For union once again with that mystic womb
The mother that was our tomb
(Ah, rest and refresh—nous a la mort) but then
I have seen it all once, and again and again
That refrain of vision is a swarm
Of stinging recollection.
And the storm!

(Out there it's *dry*—where once so wet and warm
        I harbored safely.)

For some of us the travelogue is finished.
        (What should I do in Illyria?)
One who was not my brother, but is dead—
Who had the art, almost against his will
To shadow forth a vista of delight
        By a turn of the head,
Or give, in a dappled smile
        Nearly everything,
Appalled by his own generosity, I suppose,
        Brought himself to a close.

        My brother he is in Elysium,
These eyes were no fountains fraught with tears at the funeral
        But the thirsty soul was left a little dryer
        Because of the fire
        So recently out—it's hard to discover
        What next is to be seen—what next to do
When the clerk at the information desk is by no means free
        To supply another (illustrated) guide
To lead me about these blue deep sounding beaches.
        There are so few.

Only whisper again—still hold apart:
The hand baited with love is a trap for the heart.

## *Jungle*

When our eyes were early green,
Beseech-side-up our monkey palms
        Played dumb,
And watched you pity them,
You thought because they had no thumb
        We could not use them.
You took a silly chance.
Now that our eyes are cyclamen,
We do not use our hands.

## *Old Beauty*

I who look like a monkey these days before ten
Do not particularly care if you knew me then
Or not, most of the time. Something was proven
I do not forget. Somewhere sitting by a fountain
Listening, I can get the old reflection
Of a goddess more beautiful and more mortal than anyone
Who carried in herself the secret of pleasure
Someone white and violent and small
Who smiled quietly standing naked before a mirror.
Night after night who stared stricken and silver
With love into two cold eyes, her lover
And her sun, who was told too much is forgiven
Those who are too beautiful, but who often
Laughed hearing this said. They do not know they are forgiven.
They do not know good or evil although they permit echoes,
And themselves to repeat these echoes as hostages
They give back laughing to the hungry or the living
As shadows... *it is so if you say so*... but believe me
I did not care then if you laughed or cried or bled,
And I was imperious, if you please, having one secret,
That no one else did without hunger. And you were hungry.
I commanded your rage then for my lack of appetite.
I will have no charity now for my lack of it.
You are still hungry for something you have never had,
I have had it. I can find it still when I want it.
She was my love and my nourishment.

## *Old Beauty*

God forgive me I do not any longer care
That I have broken tender habits of a hundred years
That I should hurt you touch me not at all—
No longer bless you, no longer shall conceal
From your defiant eager prurient alarm
Your fatness, thinness, your inability to dress
Your little eyes—perhaps the question of your face

No longer will I ease you, bless you, so that you with me
Become the marvelous, as if the rest of life
Had not existed, had been in error or asleep
Or victimized by fools or the very cruel

Go back to where you were; some recent year
It happened that the touch of water or sun
Could no longer please my body, nor caress…
I try to keep cool only, in the afternoons
I sleep with the shades drawn and in the evenings, rest
So soon ago your importunity
Crowding to speak to me in the theater lobby,
At the wedding or where my children learned to dance
Amused me and I was tender for you…
Aware of your pride, or your pleasure in being seen
Talking to me, of your eagerness to be known

You thought, all of you, always, that my soft hair,
The lineage of my face, my eye's felicity
Set greatly as they were in shadowy sockets
And turned to you—enough that I could tell you what you were.

I never knew what you were, perhaps never cared
Except that I was tender, and did not let you know.
Now in the evening sun I will not even listen,
I like to whine, to quarrel with my children—
I am become absorbed in the precise, the small,
Will watch a humming bird for hours, will sit still—

*Write, once and a while,*
*I'll read your letter—*
*Die, and I will not smile.*

## *[O, the little latex man]*

O, the little latex man
Cuckold his dame as cuckold can.

Bold our hero as a balloon
With eyes as motherly as a saloon,

Sucked and scooped and popped and pounded
The sky pink air which he surrounded

And billowed and boasted and poofed and wondered
Why his rubbery imminence threatened and thundered

But he flew, he flew, and none denounced him
And he bubbled the girls with his haughty bouncing

And his dame blew westerly, buried her shade,
And their heirs blew where it was wide and glad

And she smiled, she smiled, as he snuggled and snapped
And the marvelous emptiness laughed and clapped.

## *Philosopher-King*

*to Mr Rago*

Spilt the skin of the tears, the days' terrible drain,
Lopped his partial, too partial ears at the throat,
Folded the paper hands and the paper heart, opened
His notebook to the old rose folded at the comma
And climbed to and clung to the stem, a gesture
To empty his face of temptation, the tricks of the tree.

## *[What is is what was]*

What is is what was and it is there
What I am is what is here
What I will is forgot
What I would is not
And I! I am old as salt

Fruit I ate with you was less than fruit
The mango less than the pear
The pumpkin less than the paw-paw
God is older than I am but
I am older than you

This is the error of self-consciousness
That it is generally perpetuated
But usually misinterpreted
So take the silly photograph, the nasty laugh,
The vivisection of love

Oh all the similes the flesh is heir to:
Pain like mind and love like death
Sun like blood and earth like flesh
Air, the ordinary air, like breath
Only care continues cool, and now I do not care to.

## *[The rain shall rain small and hot]*

The rain shall rain small and hot
And your life be the less by one year
Before you get smart.

They don't want you and they don't want
Your advice, don't be the fool You.
Don't come between.

They want their scenery now.
The wagon man who sold them
Icecream sandwiches when they met,
Next spring they'll forget you
And remember the icecream man

## *The Bear*

For all I have to thank a lot I have
To thank THE BEAR. I think a lot of him,
I think of his dear ways and his unselfishness,
His merry gaze and his ingenious remarks
Which so enlivened our Saturday night card parties.
How he twinkled when he awarded the prizes for Hearts!
I remember his rapt paws caught in the first instance,
And the big teeth that sparkled when he talked to lawyers.
His undercoating looked vulnerable, somehow,
I used to watch it getting into taxis with a pang,
Or his gambols! Such savagery, into the wind,
But he was never cold, he said. I miss him!
I miss him! I shall never be over missing him.

## *[Why else do you have an English Horn]*

Why else do you have an English Horn if not
To blow it so I'll know to let you in.
It could be anyone, unless you do. I could be
Holding in my hand an effervescent
Preparation for the teeth, or doing swimming
Exercises on the rug, or wrapped in one,
Staring privately out the window.
                                        And I dread bagsnatchers.
Someone could be there, who would snatch my savings,
My blue glass swan I had even before I married you
All filled with quarters. Well, I can tell you,
That would be the end of our roulette games.
Therefore, use the horn, I'll never be alarmed,
I'll come at once and sing my friendly answer,
From Thaïs, you know the one, and you'll be reassured
It's me and we will both rejoice it is
The other. That is the song for which Walter Damrosch
Found so many friends in radio audiences, it goes,
WE ARE FAT GIRLS AND BOYS! WE ARE FAT GIRLS AND BOYS!
Then let not the others, delivery boys, Nosey Parkers,
Burglars, bagsnatchers or Red Feather representatives be jealous:
When you find your own true love, you will live in a house,
You too will have to have a password.

## *Whisper*

I can't whisper

But can you whistle?

Yes.

Does that surprise you?

I can tell stories.

Precious?

Very dear.

But can you whisper?

Yes.

Now we can get on with it.

Here?

Why not?

Shall it always be like this?

Not long. Already—

Yes?

Your eyes are rolling up.

It's dark here.

No, it's not.

Take his place. It is our convention.

Can you whisper?

## *[Well and you lay between the clamorous warnings]*

Well and you lay between the clamorous warnings
Soundless and without capacity for sound, the hump of buoy
Tossing unheard, on impossible oceans
Red as a bell and white as a chicken feather,
Round, round, so self contained
        that snuffy perjury of dreams could not awake you
        nor twitch your eyelid to reprisal in the sun
        nor pluck the soon forgetful, dull bedraggled nerve
        nor yet engender resolution in the bone.
We are fickle to the fast water of our indulgence,
We are wet where we would be dry and no better,
We are dream where we would be incontinent,
Inconsistent where it could hardly matter more...
        assume the bathhouse spectacle of the parasol,
        the beach, the heat, the wet sand stuck to skin,
        the genial brazen smart of sand, the drop of wind
        all parenthetically officiate the sun.

## *[what hours, love]*

what hours, love, what hours lie
critical and silently
in all we see
        the ice brown folds of the running river
        snow clouds
        all light's ministry, anguish to our memory
        piercing the private vision, promising recall
        the eyes of animals

where were we, what did we
before we were critical
between the time of innocence and grief
when all our gestures froze, polemical,
into attitudes
and we forever wondering what they were
        once I think we ran
        slapped by the wind at once
        sun filled
        powered with burst breathing
        into everything we did
        everywhere
        one attention
looked neither forward nor back but violent
performed on top of sleep and then fell back
soundless and without chagrin
until the morning forced us eagerness

## *At Harvard Bridge*

Stop the car, draw up here,
Here by remembered motion
Torn by the river light where fear
Subsides behind us, no closer:

Begin all over again and tell me.
*Something moves beneath me, squirms*
*And struggles to get out; I am afraid.*

What moves? *Water beneath me,*
*Earth, flesh, the seasons—everything unseen.*

There was the traffic, the spoils
Of falling overrode us: Here
Observe the shore, the purpose,
The bridge that hangs before us like a sneer.

Even the floorboards shudder, start,
Then by my kicking could I open silence
Revealing violence? Our shell
Explode and throw us upwards?
*Trust no moving part.*

Clouds, storms, the heavy thrust of heart
Pushing against the flesh beside you,
Fear it, fear it; it may find you
Helpless against it, giddy, ill.

We'll not drive on together. Early rain
Will fall, the light will fail again,
The darkness take us with uncertainty;
I cannot drive you home, I do not know the way.

Somewhere you sleep in a closet, eat for comfort,
Read at your solitary meals, somewhere
Make curious secret faces in a secret room,
Somewhere you speak with panic to a telephone,
And there I'll find you when you want to speak.

*But look, look, the sun devoured the water.*
*Rest no longer here, the river burns.*

Sunset my plight of ridicule, my empty hands
And my damp rag arms, peace:
Even the stone see miracles, tease them with their eyes,
Their prayers are only for conviction. Now beneath

The lowering pitch of sky your black mouth hides
In shadow by a snarl the dread of miracles:

*Save me, save me, who will not be saved;*
*Move me, who will break you if you do;*
Then if you cannot, come, conform—
Lie trapped into my ice as bits of fern,
Footprint, fur and claw imprinted here
Useless, ageless, immemorial.

We'll go, for now it's still,
In false light for a compromise.

## *[So lean to your caress]*

So lean to your caress,
The light went through me, and bent,
Somehow, turned out and disappeared

Angel of the efficacious surrender
Procured at the bent of my smile like
A curled prong, what is that ship they always
Talk of that went down? Some holy where no crow
Can reach unless he sails. That was my crow,
The one who could not fly.

Verisimilarly I
Stroked the water and looked down
Into a pale brown world I could not fathom.

## *Reaching Out Our Hands to One Another (Bedbugs)*

Take heart, we are not alone:
For all of time, I am certain,
People who would otherwise be sleeping
Have found one, at least one
        And wrapped them
        In paper to say to someone
        *Is this one?*
They lie on their backs with their legs overhead
When they are dead and they turn red.
Nothing ever happened, no matter what,
So terrible that we had it
When someone else did not.
        Just remember that.
        Take comfort.

## *Torturing*

While you were beating an
Improving article in a review

Your face squeezed-up and
Nervous and your head crouched
Like a heavy ball in its socket
Well I kicked up
All the fur of feathers and moths
And the blanket cover snowed up
And over how furious you were

Stop stop those awful hands like birds
You said, nipping and where it tore
The collar button, stop you kicked
And bellowed in a bull-like bell
Tone thrashing down

My bad black barefoot foot the instep
Up got under the small
Of your back and whack, went your
Review which landed on the floor
Across the room, my pinching hands
Went after you, you could not get
Into the iced fruit or the milk,
I would not let you

Pots fell down, pans, glasses
Clanked and shivered watch out
Watch out I cried the telephone
The clock the glasses and the pans
Watch out your watch my wrist

I broke last winter, don't kick
Don't thrash THEN

My eye you hit lit up
Like scalding suns, and spun,
And then went blurred, my rage
Rubbed out the clock, its glass bell
Shimmered out of focus I kicked
Up and thrust back and washed
And wouldn't speak, how cross
I was. And you were
In disgrace. You said
How awful you had been
and how I should be cross
And I said, yes.

## *And Hang a Calfskin on Those Recreant Limbs*

Who ate the poisoned chicken, you? No.
It's I who've poison in my thighs.
It's I who's strung on chicken bones, and I, it was,
That gobbled up the poison. I'm flying.
You, you're dying just because you're chicken. Why
Are you painting crucifixions? That's
What you said, didn't you, not chickens?
I heard about you tearing off to the Bosphorus,
That way, to eat grass. Now, just what was
Nebuchadnezzar's story? Was he like us?
Did he have to get down on his hands and knees to
Roar like a lion, WHAT YOU DON'T UNDERSTAND IS
I'M NOT A MAN AND I CAN'T, oh I can see you
Sitting with your Turkish friends, blowing their fuses,
Splicing their cables, crawling under their pipe lines
But the Turks had gods too, first some,
And then some other ones. Will they take you, too,
I wonder, even though you are taller than they are?
That's it, isn't it, Nebuchadnezzar? it's easier
To be a god than human, you never get off the ground.
                                        I don't care what you do.
After I detached my toenails one by one, I sat down
In the loudest sun with a good book to wait for the poison
To take command, Kutkutkedaddle cut
Shrieked that sweaty setting Brahmin. I came on
Like a concupiscent tiger all oranges when I found that
in King John (when your loins are rotten with
Industrial dust and machine parings you've got
To sit still and move your eyes as if it hadn't
Happened)          *thou wear a lion's skin?*

## *[To rhythmically grind our jaws]*

To rhythmically grind our jaws, marvelous,
It is a battalion going before sense.
Behind this steady chewing I am impervious
As a *donna* laid down at noon behind the sun.
Now I know I'll marry and it won't matter.
O Turkish baths! Melt me. No one cares.
Believe me, were it not for the Convention
That undergoes, no shows should take place,
But unreally these shows shall face to face
Show and show. Beware the bear that chases
From June to December, beware the holes in the ice!

## *[This time, what are the conditions of cowardice?]*

This time, what are the conditions of cowardice?
A stranger bathing in the sea survived a snail…
Through all these multifarious generations I have had one idea
I have had it sick or well.

                                        Let the snail say now what he can,
The sun leaves the beach like the tide itself, the playing waters
Soda bright and mineral. Hitches to the sticking sand grass
Stroking the dunes. I lay away all day. A burnt match
Six feet away at my cold feet my eyes feasted bodily

Time and enough to write YOU when the weather gets holy
Reports from the sacristy now conflict with the open press
Journalists are to be seen knitting their eyebrows
                                        into sweaters for park benches
Seen in the park: only shoes, shoes for as far as the eye can trust itself
Time enough for comprisals when the weather is fair
And the lily light splashes out a monument from the mouths of horses
In equestrian statues. The spring makes bad.

                                        Out of what fen did your mother come, little
                                        bark-the-shin, was she competent, like you?

## *Notes on Solitude*

"Attir'd with Stars, we shall for ever sit,
Triumphing over Death, and Chance, and thee O Time."
—John Milton

There are not minutes in time only words
And the words inverts in all shame naked
Without their clothes on. When minutes cease
The words cease also.

In Franz Josef Land, in Spitsbergen
I lay down and wept.
In Grahamland I lost my right arm,
Bitten by frost. (Oh, had I loved that loneliness!)
Spitzbergen, waste-wild wilderness,
If I forget thee let me keep my cunning!

So I, maze-wild, walk sillyfooted
In a now wilderness of frosted crystal
Faces like burnt out electric light bulbs.
Oh Lord, Lord, give me back the use of my right arm.

## *[Somewhere he not anywhere no]*

Somewhere he not anywhere no
In such a place this anywhere he
Is monumental as monuments go.

In that excision,
In that chaste climate,
Look well who hopes well
that fall is a long fall.

Oh, devil take Mary and pluck out her fingernails,
I am a stuck site and the laws of the land are binding.
Pick up your fence wire and the cords of delivery,
I am not pleading a choice, I have forgiven that.

Agnes wet-her-bed. Her mother has perceived it.
Agnes dreamt of a beast she never saw.

## *Travelling South*

1
Before we crossed from the Eastern Shore
Into Virginia we stopped and saw
Broccoli growing in the middle of winter
In the middle of nowhere. By a gas station.

                                        We asked the man
How it grew, and how it came to ripen,
For it was full grown, the sky so grey,
The weather, so he said, sometimes to twenty.
                                        He didn't know.
It was the first green thing that we saw grow.

We can escape from greed and fear.
If it is here, in the car,
It will not be far
Before it can no longer find us.
We three, separately,
Will be more than we are,
Will be less than we were.
Together we are,
Separate we will be.
We will taste, touch, and see,
We three.

We will learn the pleasures of our irresponsibilities.
Miss Steele will play cards. Jack could do worse,
and I will do things ten times important as
I ever did. Everything will be changed.

2

In Dover, Delaware, I went to sleep
At once, in our Motel. But Miss Steele
Stayed angrily awake, turned to the wall.
Next day she said she had to sleep alone.
I smiled. And so she did, in New Berne.
We called no names, but all the day between,
Jack wondered what had happened.
No one knew. Not she, not I, not he,
But three strangers.

Cigarette signs in North Carolina:
Growers bring your tobacco here.
Snuff on sale, and incomprehensible
Voices quoting prices.
A lady in the street spoke to me,
In a queer quiet town: "It's this wind,
Everybody's down sick." Miss Steele went to look
At antiques, I walked on the street,
Jack went into a public rest-room.

New Berne was older than God.
Tree or stump or cow.
Something lived here we did not know,
Secret and grave. In our house
We were shown where, in the Civil War,
Yankees lived there, under barricade.
They were pleased to have us,
The mother, who sold antiques,
The father, who liked to talk,
And the daughter, a tough blonde nurse
Whose stockings, and drying uniform
Hung in our bathroom. I slept, wondering why
This house made me so queer when I came in it.

Miss Steele became more tense,
Gaped like an old fish, her bulging eyes
Glancing over the back seat.
"Jack had a terrible night.
I couldn't sleep, because of the noise.
You, I suppose, made out all right."
I said I did. I knew now, how
She hated me. For what? For reading
In the back seat, for detachment,
For reading while I ate.
For talking cheerfully with Jack.
For all the reasons we came South to lose.
And then, I had seen her in her corset,
I had seen her put on rouge.
She could scarcely forgive me for that.
Oh Miss Steele, Miss Steele, it was my fault.
You could not accept what you saw, reflected.

In Savannah: "Jack is sick.
He's going to a doctor.
Jack is *very* sick. We must be tactful,
And show him every consideration that we can."
Jack found a dentist. He disappeared
Into the louvered, interlocking squares
For hours. Savannah! We pushed through Spanish moss,
Hung from great trees, and drove into a city
Of wonders. There at last came the tears.

## *[Would she improve]*

Would she improve
By despair? Would she move
To stroke the strange
Dog? Would she do it?

Now her head is the size of a walnut,
Cold and hazardous the eyes drop out
To see the qualities of self about.

## *[I have no memory for beginnings]*

I have no memory for beginnings, or for cause;
The snow's betrayal, the early fruits of thaw
Were all I called the chilly similar years
To hatred for, now all I do is all I knew
Of winter, all I learned to do; now all I hope
Is peace, or place to celebrate in ways
My summer's ghostly anniversaries.

We had no memory of cause, but there were those
Who said they knew, and these were wrong;
The hobble-mouthed of crippled tongue
Were true, who had no heart for song,
Too old for what they tried to do
Too tired to suppose.

## *[The pines pull up from their needles]*

The pines pull up from their needles
The white sky covers like a scar
The whiter day beyond
At four pm they're on their way
Asking no questions from the car
The road into the mountain leads
Up, with a thousand signs
The white line wavers and weaves
On a dark road bounded by autumn leaves
You, your eyes growing anxious in the car
With the curtain ring on your finger,
Life is full of error, yours
Will not be very deep or very long.

## *Letter from Grandma Morning*

And to you maidens, cretins, counterpatriots,
Grow wise with compromise, my adjurations end in time:
Await no dreaded moment, praying, *everything depends on this*,
The cumulative act, as cumulative seconds fall
And leave the naked face to stunned dismay;
Make no attachments, abandon the symbolic inference,
Disregard your precious drama, pretend that it is someone else.
Make no mistake of ever finding how that you might also fail;
Never, never sell unless you do not need to make the sale.

## *Ultra-Violet*

Gulls describe a sidereal arc
Between six and seven o'clock
In the new day
Still drunk at seven at six
Awake to watch the river pitch
Toy cars play
Below in the planed austerities
Highway, river, gulls, cars, all grey
Like the last stars
Sleep again
Before the light starts burning
Holes in the white room

## *Money and Time*

Today I noticed I have four clocks in my room and all of them are broken.

1\.
Clocks clocks clocks, I don't know when
I'll understand your poem. I know I have to. "Dear Helen"
I write Tuesday, "Yesterday is coming."
Still pond, no more moving.
Why does your poem have a happy ending?

2\.
Bridges run under rivers under rivers, they are
All the same in time, the Mantuan's scars,
Cigar-butt burns, have scaled and they will heal.
Mantuan Cantabrigian or at your house, it was all the same,
Still pond. Very still. Is that a sestina? Yours, I mean.

3\.
He walks on broken bridges. (He was my nurse.
He came to me with plans for public buildings
And careful drafts for longer poems in Latin.
I said Take Everything, I did a rowdy tap-dance
On the first broken bridge. Just to remind you.)
Bridges hesitate before their own reflection,
Then break at centre to go back where they came from.
If you want my broken clocks, just send for them!
Still pond, I have my hip boots on,
Can we ever change anything? Here is a nursery rhyme.
Dry clocks in upper rooms
Beat between the cage bones
Remember us
When blood boiled over on your stove
And how we fussed!

But clocks still break beneath the skin,
To tell time, clock by water.
I wonder.
Clocks, clocks, clocks. I will read it a hundred times.
Our heads have halves—one half accepts no questions.

4.

Wednesday. Dear Helen, When
All our fingernails are dimes
Our eyes will rage and tell like silver dollars!
Gleam and prove. You wait. Our energy will move
The underground and pull the subways. Clocks then
(At night sometimes I hear them) in revolution
Will beat their hands like ostrich wings and run
Headless across the dry canals. We always wanted answers!
Our tears will drop from chewing-gum machines like pennies
And buy the power lines—will even silver mirrors,
Will rivet bridges and instruct the laborers
To love, will open locks will span canals will fill the dry ponds!
Oh they which are so useless now will then be precious.
*All this is when he comes.*
We are so helpless,
Our senses never spend and never purchase.
Is this, do you suppose, why these clocks can no longer move?

5.

But I have bled my poor tears in every traffic policeman's
stained white glove
And I have mailed my head in every open letter box and listened
To the round mouth form—falling—a whispered
O for love,
I have waited hour after hour at the carrier cotes—
It must return, the gay official dove,
It will be bringing bread and money, it will teach me how to read.

## *[Shall we remember this year]*

Shall we remember this year as one
In which we were happy and well?
Letters are deceptive; thoughts disappear;
The twisted heart permits erasure
Of all but the promissory instant.
We are startled to recollect that, here,
We were so very much the same, so sure
Of distance put behind us, our own growth.
Could we have come, so hurtfully, so far
Only to this instant where, we now admit, we are?

## *Poems to Preserve the Years at Home*

i.

First Year

Cocktail party. It takes all day to dress.
Thinking about it. Eat. Wash. Finally
The exquisite touches, employing Choice.
To this one I'll wear pale green silk stockings

They'll be nothing but poets there. Or the writers
Of terse short stories. One celebrity.
Catch as catch can. A green silk handkerchief too.

This is Miss Lang, Miss V. R. Lang. The Poet, or
The Poetess...                Bynum, would you introduce
Someone else as          this is J. P. Hatchet
Who is a Roman Catholic?          No. Then don't do
That to me again. It's not an employment,
It's a private religion. Who's that over there?

What do you want me to say then?
—what an illogical position!—
This is V. R. Lang, she lives at home?

She lives at home, she lives at home.
She knows how to play backgammon
No bridge, no canasta
Likes to drive in her car
Has had two accidents so far
And two poems published this year
Two, the first two, in May
And who cares anyway. Bynum, and one other,

A hopeless ass who has a bigger car and a nasty fetish
About the way I wear my hair.
All his girls wear their
Hair the way I do, I see from snapshots.
We'll see about that. Come August
I'll cut it all off and wear it very short.

Come unto me, you friends of my childhood
Who still remain, and we'll try it again.
Jack, who still is
A contemporary and Bob
Who is good for the movies.
*Violet always picks the hits*
He said bitterly, after my last outrageous choice.

Letters to friends:
I get these continual colds...
I forgot to ask, did you pass your reading exams?
It's curious. I don't seem to be able to accomplish
*Anything*. Everything begun. Nothing ever finished.
Heaps and piles of waste.... How is Keith...
Not that I give a good God Damn. No man
Is going to make me suffer ever again.

*Put it in the corner with the unmailed letters*

We learn ONE THING,
Simple statement can't afford release.
It has got to be something
Bewildering. Complicated. Preferably
Mysterious to the self at time of writing.

Woke up at four
Muttering aloud
*Scarlet flavor*

*Drop scarlet*
*Not a bit of crystal*
Something like that.
Peculiar. It affords comfort.

No adumbration then. No journalistic writing.
That way Hell lies, gaping wide open and inviting
Saying Come in and forget everything you meant.
Everything you started eager out to do.

No numbers. No lists. No categoricals.
No descriptive adjectives. BURN IT OUT.
TEAR IT OUT. Attempt no descriptions.
Talk about flames. Suicides. Terror in sleep.

ii.

No use, no use. The immovable
Outdoors… I'm suffocating here
But I can't move my hands… the pile
Of papers on the floor… the unmailed letters

The rival systems, each out to catch
The morning's mail or the bills
So what. So they get put on bureaus.
I'll never find them when the time comes.
But all around me boxes, papers, papers, drawers
Files… filing cabinets... especial drawers

The typewriter which jams. The voice downstairs
That calls. The telephone which enters.
The emergency. The caller. The hot water heater that breaks.
I can't remember        I can't remember
I put something here        I had something to do

Someone to telephone, some letter to answer
If I write about this bill, will they let me alone?
The TABLED overwhelming accumulations

I tried to beat the air
I went to walk instead
But little gnats flew around my head
It was desolate, walking alone
Talking to no one
Thinking, seeing me like this
Walking, talking to myself
That couple will have said I'm queer

Can't make two letters come together right
On this damnable machine. Something is ALWAYS wrong
Nothing ever quite works, or is ready to wear

For five months those shoes have waited for repair
In a paper bag which says, cobbler
For two months a hat to be steamed and blocked

How much money has gone into that car
To get me out of here?

I'll never go. I'll walk the floors at home
Until there is no longer any room in my room.
Pictures, papers, papers, books. Letters. Things to wear.
Piles of clothing on the chairs. Burnt-out electric bulbs.
Forgotten appliances like a polishing tool.
Directions to work the polishing tool.
In three different places as a rule.

If the telephone rings, will I have the strength to say no?

iii.

Spent late last night with stinking brigands,
Who capered through my sleep like dirty clowns
Committing a murder in the early morning
How should I know whose. I woke up frowning, and
Murderous too. I saw a monkey out my window
At noon. I bruised my elbow jumping through.
How many times have I taken those stairs saying,
It won't be long now? My promises squeak and sneak
Like dreaming burglars scheming in their sleep.

iv.

All day I sat in the room alone
All day I looked at a wide white wall
I slept through the dentist, I stayed at home    (broke an appointment)

I stayed and I stared at a fingernail
Now I stare at a bird in a tree
Outside my window, he's singing to me

Accidie, accidie, acci-dee dee dee

He isn't a bird like the birds I've known
And I've been places, and I've seen birds

v.

The Narcosis doesn't sleep and never reads.
It eats. It feeds and feeds
On everything that happens.

First year summer, Ohio. For twelve hours
On the train that marvelous sensation
Of falling into place with all one's wits working.
Coming alive and cooking, everything made sense
And moved and shuddered and smoked. I wrote a letter
To poor Milton about that awful Confession, even
A poem. What I mean, I followed him. That didn't
Comfort me when it was published because he shouldn't.
But I followed him. In that kind of suspension
With the wind behind, anything is possible,
Like being a person. It stopped at Mt. Vernon.
I flopped like a fish a few times driving in the car
That wood accentuated state road to Gambier.
Oh, God. Gambier. Like being buried up to your neck.
The valley low and moist and steamy and growing immense,
Queen Anne's Lace seven feet tall with trunks like snakes,
Grass squirming, ground squashy, the air filled with flying gnats.
Horrible bird noises and distant shrieks. At night,
In the next house, lying awake, I listened for monkeys.
The sun couldn't get through the hot wet air. Some hours
I dragged a chair and a table out into the afternoon
And tried to write, it was futile, bugbitten and overwhelming.
I'd walk to the postoffice hoping for the afternoon mail
And get Brad's 8 page unwanted daily letter
*When are you coming home* sentimental fat and spurious
Or Margie's hysterical notes. I wrote Jackson,
Wildly upset, tangled by her in the octopus arms,
Panicky and defensive, *what have I done now*
Margie answered he thinks you're no help around the house.
Bug's Black Blood. I wrote awful letters all night
And got up too tired to live, or listen to Angie.

Fletcher was born, and almost died, and we held the service
All three of us struggling not to cry when he was baptised

For the black journey he'd have to make without us. We'd known
Him such a little while. All the awful jocularity
That goes with having a baby came nevertheless to Don.
The man in the general store, the man in the restaurant.
Don't say anything to her, Don said, in case he doesn't make it.
Amy looked bewildered. She was two. But he pulled through
And I was his godmother, I'll always be glad of that.

vi.

(and that leaves
        theatrical gestures...)

Back where I belong. The disorder
Is my own, it can't spring
At me, or break out weeping,
Or explode. The grey windows
Have this to be said for them,
It does not matter what shows
If no one else knows, or is watching
Critically, head cocked in a little sneer.
There is no one like that here.
When the stove works, it is warm,
And despite it does not, it is comfortable
Enough to stare in, lie down in,
Or look at an opposite wall. It isn't
All so grey. There are magic areas
Some of them in the past, some of them
In the mind. Some sitting on chairs, in scrapbooks,
In the closet. Magic enough for the one who left them.

        Called up, they corrupt or create
        Of real (or disagreeable) images something
        Workable. These are to live with. Or learn by.

How to do something not wanted to do, don't.
Clouds make grey swans in the air. The heart pumps
A little pallor, a little fever, the third sister,
Hypocrisy, stands apart. Fear is not bad,
Nor an experience of tears trying out the stillness

vii.

Winter birds, willow sitting winter birds
Peer through the window which is darker than the day
Accidie, accidie, dee, dee dee.

In a witch bright day I had no one to play
With and which-stared and a which white wall
Where I hung by a fingernail, no one called
And no one came, then 25 times I wrote my name
Under 25 broken appointments, always the same
Name and sometimes the same appointments. If you
Were taller and stronger and truly true
And called me a wonder, I know what I'd do.

I'd go to the dentist, I'd wind all the clocks
I'd plug in the telephone back by its box
I'd answer the letters I get sometimes
I'd pick up my clothes where I throw them nights
I'd sort my papers and keep them on file
I'd save some money once in a while
If you loved me and if I loved you
(This is a conceit rather than an observation)

viii.

Look George you told me
The bottom's gone back when you're tempted
To turn (black and holy)
                                        Out of hindsight
                                        Earshot or record
                                        Into No One.
That the swallows of love are the light
Flying wisely where they know
No one will say I told you so

Because between No One and Love lies You
And between You and No One such weeping
As rocks the walls of your heart and crushes your ribs
Coming to nothing, believing in nothing believable
Sure and yet unsure, wicked and yet lovely

And between You and Love lies perjury, pride
The testament of Use, the savagery of magic

There's you standing black and huge and foreign
Crossed against the sky like a canyon
Crooked into the light like a tree

I think I know the No One
Wearing your oldest clothes and
Eager to work and dedicated and
Prayer and composure and beautiful accomplishment
(I shall get away, once alone,
I shall be Love itself, no I
Shall block peace, my purpose)
Is indeed Love, and before that terrible reckoning
You stand committed, barring all passage.

ix.

I don't want to dream of the dead man again, I don't
Want to wake up wanting to go back to sleep. Somebody
Take me that I can believe in before everything…
I am tired of those tired names, I never had my parents,
I never        the wind with a tomato tongue        bears down
Upon the wind        there is no breath between
But two angered storm heads in a void

If it is you, little and pale,
God give me back the thunder I lost

If I had hunger once I have eaten it.
God give me the skin I was born with,
My eyes are bled and my fingers fat
Everywhere I went to tonight
Said, the end is coming. Middle age
Is like that. Not here or there but violent.
If I had... what. Revenge. But revenge is
Never wholly personal. It could count, like fortune,
For anyone.        God grant
Something perfect. You know what
I mean by that…

x.

The one into the other creeps,
The touching world into the word,
The gesture parts the lips,
The boundaries are found and stared.

The gesture trips the careful tongue;
The eyelids catch, the eye is heard.

xi.

Up till then I had never thought of my life
As a waking attitude, finite and calculable,
No more does one walk on the earth and under the sky
Attending the over all and constricting dimension.
You live in, you do not question, a master plan.

If life is measurable the system falls apart,
To try or to start causing fearful pain of conscience
And sleepless planning. *Not to finish* becomes the challenge.
Grey eagles in the air beat at sleep. The nightime radio
Becomes a drug, fanning out through the tragic worries.
Those concerns trivial and meaningless become luxuries
Beloved for themselves, but they grow fewer, very few.

There must be things to remember that were perfect
Or at least proud, but they are riddled with doubts
And humiliation now. What could have contented us?
They were half done, they were luck, they were accidents
We cannot now lean on them or be sure that they were enough.
Days too, days are filled with hopeless unfulfillment,
Things forgotten return to haunt the bed at night,
Merciless errands and important purposes all day all week lain dormant
Now to spring from crouched positions into persecution
Too the tongue claw.

xii.

Tuesday when you opened your eyes your
Room was a cold disaster, arranged
Around you, its own disorderly life

Took stock of you like a crazy pendulum
Swung over your head like a demonstration
In a science museum, your hands were numb

All the pieces of you clung to the bedclothes
Like a broken promise, sorrow sticking to the cracks
Till you sat up and the floor went dizzy

You did not go near the mirror, you fed the cat
But it went on weeping, and you had to sit down

Still all that day you were followed by your
Tall still angels, walking like trees
You had no choice but to lead them, and twice

You listened, and once, you smiled.

Some days the days for providence we wake
Up taller than the telephone, our eyes more harsh and black
And even its screaming cannot shock us

Somedays we wake up to the Act
Which casts a shadow on the infinite plane
Of suggestion, we become our Agents

Pay our rent and sort the laundry
Make appointments, go to market,
Lay in stores with strange, beleaguered haste

Some days our guardian days we
Go gladly into one dimension;
These days our days are not our dominion

But our deliverance, practical and moral,
On these days only motion casts a shadow

xiii.

Well and he said I will, I
WILL, the rest is chance. My cat's
Ears were cut down. Young, the live ones
Burst all over the bed and were photographed,
I sat by without pain. I will not be taken
naked, I refuse to be a monument. The ears,
Being plaster, were chipped. I will live
as close to the idea as I can command!
You are in error, you will snarl like cutweed.
Bill, leaving Brussels, asked
The merchant who kept him, what keep.
Now going back, he said,
What can I send you that I spent?
And the merchant said,
*Quelquechoses de permanent.*
*But what to me, my love? but what*
*to me?* Well for these three, one
An incapacity, a lie, an antique failure
I wish you disaster, nothing permanent.

xiv.

Before you accept life, make no mistake,
Those that can give life can take it back.
Those that can bring you to life can take,
In their taking, more than thy brought.
This since we learned we could eat without appetite.
Powers go still, time runs out, God I am so tired.
There is only the black center in my head
To reconstruct, to ache, to take dictation.

I never once thought about death
Before I started to die. Time grows thin.
The animal arts are turning from pleasure to pain.
I told you everything before you slept, and lay awake
To bite my tongue which knew, which always knew
That what is finally spoken is no longer true.
And you had only listened till I told you.

## *[A terror to love what death can take]*

A terror to love what death can take,
A terror to take what death can touch,
A terror to touch what is taken too late
Knowing what was taken must be kept
And what is kept cannot be taken.

A terror to touch what lives to die
That which is not token but is temporized,
That which is not taken but tampered with
Beyond all power of its execution
taken, tested, trusted, twisted, turned, adumbrated, telescoped tarnished tangled
shivered shot kaleidoscoped caught shot hung

carnage

Cry

## *[If you passed unharmed through the miraculous season]*

If you passed unharmed through the miraculous season,
What now when the year runs out with chattering of teeth?
The embroidery unfinished, the pile of unmailed letters,
The echo in the empty well, what can they tell you?

The spider in the grate, the empty, indifferent weather
May be a clue. But better not to know.

# *Acknowledgements*

I am beyond delighted that Bunny has found a place at New York Review Books, and I want to extend my sincerest gratitude to Edwin Frank, Alex Andriesse, Sara Kramer, and Abigail Dunn—and everyone else at NYRB—for their patience, generosity and enthusiasm. I also want to thank everyone at Carcanet (particularly Michael Schmidt, John McAuliffe, Jazmine Linklater, and Andrew Latimer), who originally brought *The Miraculous Season* to life in its UK edition.

Without the support and encouragement of Sayre Phillips Sheldon, V. R. Lang's sister-in-law, this work would never have been published. Sadly, Sayre passed away in Cambridge, on September 28, 2025—her ninety-ninth birthday. She always welcomed me into her home with astonishing generosity and warmth, and I will always be grateful to her for this, and for her kind permission to publish Lang's writing. For this edition, Sayre's daughter Alexandra Sheldon has offered invaluable assistance and enlivening advocacy; I could not be more thankful to her and look forward to finally meeting!

I would like to extend my boundless thanks to the Houghton Library at Harvard, particularly the archivists and librarians who patiently brought me box after box, day after day, on multiple trips since 2018. I'm sorry I'm always picky about getting the sharpest pencil. I am especially grateful to the Houghton for awarding me the 2023/2024 Joan Nordell Visiting Fellowship, an honour that enabled much of this editorial undertaking. Work on this book was also made possible thanks to a British Academy Postdoctoral Fellowship.

I am indebted to the many people and organisations who have aided and abetted my Bunny Lang obsession over the years, including—but not limited to—the Network for New York School Studies (particularly Rona Cran and Yasmine Shamma), the indefatigable and brilliant Nick Sturm, Daniel Kane, Patrick Errington, Oli Hazzard, Don Paterson, and my beloved colleagues in the School of English at the University of St Andrews. I also want to acknowledge the work and generosity of Allison Vanouse, who has kept warm the embers of Lang's legacy in recent years.

Moss Pepe, Alexa Winik, and Becky Birrell all saw haphazard early versions of this book, and offered inestimable opinions and advice, as well as love and friendship that I will attempt to spend forever repaying. Gratitude for emotional support is also due to my little household god: Scout the dog.

I am lucky beyond measure to have my agent, Harriet Moore. Thank you for championing Bunny and me.

Thank you to Frank, for pointing the way.

And thank you to Bunny—send a bird if you like it.

Other versions of some of these poems were previously published in *The Pitch* (1962); *V. R. Lang: Poems & Plays, with A Memoir by Alison Lurie* (1975); *Poetry*; *Quarterly Review of Literature; i.e. The Cambridge Review*; *Folder*; *The New Pocket Anthology of Modern Verse*; *Chicago Review*; *Semi-Colon*; and *Measure*.

# *Index of Poem Titles*

**DANTE ALIGHIERI** The New Life
*Translated by Dante Gabriel Rossetti; Preface by Michael Palmer*

**KINGSLEY AMIS** Collected Poems: 1944–1979

**YURI ANDRUKHOVYCH** Set Change
*Translated by Ostap Kin and John Hennessy*

**ANTONELLA ANEDDA** Historiae
*Translated by Patrizio Ceccagnoli and Susan Stewart*

**GUILLAUME APOLLINAIRE** Zone: Selected Poems
*Translated by Ron Padgett*

**AUSTERITY MEASURES** The New Greek Poetry
*Edited by Karen Van Dyck*

**CHARLES BAUDELAIRE** Flowers of Evil
*Translated by George Dillon and Edna St. Vincent Millay*

**HAYIM NAHMAN BIALIK** On the Slaughter
*Translated and with an introduction by Peter Cole*

**SZILÁRD BORBÉLY** Berlin-Hamlet
*Translated by Ottilie Mulzet*

**SZILÁRD BORBÉLY** In a Bucolic Land
*Translated by Ottilie Mulzet*

**ANDRÉ BRETON AND PHILIPPE SOUPAULT**
The Magnetic Fields
*Translated by Charlotte Mandel*

**MARGARET CAVENDISH** *Edited by Michael Robbins*

**PAUL CELAN** Letters to Gisèle
*Translated by Jason Kavett*

**AMIT CHAUDHURI** Sweet Shop: New and Selected Poems, 1985–2023

**NAJWAN DARWISH** Exhausted on the Cross
*Translated by Kareem James Abu-Zeid; Foreword by Raúl Zurita*

**NAJWAN DARWISH** Nothing More to Lose
*Translated by Kareem James Abu-Zeid*

**FARNOOSH FATHI** Granny Cloud

**BENJAMIN FONDANE** Cinepoems and Others
*Edited by Leonard Schwartz*

**GLORIA GERVITZ** Migrations: Poem, 1976–2020
*Translated by Mark Schafer*

**ZUZANNA GINCZANKA** Firebird
*Translated by Alissa Valles*

**PERE GIMFERRER** *Translated by Adrian Nathan West*

**W. S. GRAHAM** *Selected by Michael Hofmann*

**SAKUTARŌ HAGIWARA** Cat Town
*Translated by Hiroaki Sato*

**MICHAEL HELLER** Telescope: Selected Poems

**MIGUEL HERNÁNDEZ** *Selected and translated by Don Share*

**EMMANUEL HOCQUARD** Elegies
*Translated by Cole Swensen*

**RICHARD HOWARD** RH ♥ HJ and Other American Writers
*Introduction by Timothy Donnelly*

**RYSZARD KRYNICKI** Our Life Grows
*Translated by Alissa Valles; Introduction by Adam Michnik*

**LOUISE LABÉ** Love Sonnets and Elegies
*Translated by Richard Sieburth*

**V. R. "BUNNY" LANG** The Miraculous Season
*Edited by Rosa Campbell*

**LI SHANGYIN** *Edited and translated by Chloe Garcia Roberts*

**AT THE LOUVRE** Poems by 100 Contemporary World Poets

**OSIP MANDELSTAM** Voronezh Notebooks
*Translated by Andrew Davis*

**ARVIND KRISHNA MEHROTRA** *Selected by Vidyan Ravinthiran; Introduction by Amit Chaudhuri*

**HENRI MICHAUX** A Certain Plume
*Translated by Richard Sieburth; Preface by Lawrence Durrell*

**MELISSA MONROE** Medusa Beach

**EUGENIO MONTALE** Late Montale
*Selected and translated by George Bradley*

**CHRISTIAN MORGENSTERN** The Gallows Songs
*Translated by Max Knight; Introduction by Samuel Titan*

**JOAN MURRAY** Drafts, Fragments, and Poems: The Complete Poetry
*Edited and with an introduction by Farnoosh Fathi; Preface by John Ashbery*

**ÁLVARO MUTIS** Maqroll's Prayer and Other Poems
*Translated by Chris Andrews, Edith Grossman, and Alastair Reid*

**VIVEK NARAYANAN** After

**SILVINA OCAMPO** *Selected and translated by Jason Weiss*

**EUGENE OSTASHEVSKY** The Feeling Sonnets

**EUGENE OSTASHEVSKY** The Pirate Who Does Not Know the Value of Pi
*Art by Eugene and Anne Timerman*

**ELISE PARTRIDGE** The If Borderlands: Collected Poems

**CESARE PAVESE** Hard Labor
*Translated by William Arrowsmith; afterword by Ted Olson*

**DAVID PLANTE** The Death of a Greek Lover

**VASKO POPA** *Selected and translated by Charles Simic*

**J.H. PRYNNE** The White Stones
*Introduction by Peter Gizzi*

**ALICE PAALEN RAHON** Shapeshifter
*Translated and with an introduction by Mary Ann Caws*

**A. K. RAMANUJAN** The Interior Landscape: Classical Tamil Love Poems

**PIERRE REVERDY** *Edited by Mary Ann Caws*

**DENISE RILEY** Say Something Back & Time Lived, Without Its Flow

**ARTHUR RIMBAUD** The Drunken Boat: Selected Writings
*Edited by Mark Polizzotti*

**STEPHEN RODEFER** Four Lectures

**AMELIA ROSSELLI** Sleep

**JACK SPICER** After Lorca
*Preface by Peter Gizzi*

**THE TEN THOUSAND LEAVES** Poems from the Man'yōshū
*Translated by Ian Hideo Levy*

**MARINA TSVETAEVA** Three by Tsvetaeva
*Translated by Andrew Davis*

**CÉSAR VALLEJO,** Trilce
*Translated and with glosses by William Rowe and Helen Dimos*

**ALEXANDER VVEDENSKY** An Invitation for Me to Think
*Translated by Eugene Ostashevsky and Matvei Yankelevich*

**WANG YIN** A Summer Day in the Company of Ghosts
*Translated by Andrea Lingenfelter*

**WALT WHITMAN** Drum-Taps: The Complete 1865 Edition
*Edited by Lawrence Kramer*

**NACHOEM M. WIJNBERG** *Translated by David Colmer*

**LAKDHAS WIKKRAMASINHA**
*Edited by Michael Ondaatje and Aparna Halpé*

**ELIZABETH WILLIS** Alive: New and Selected Poems

**ZHENG XIAOQIONG** In the Roar of the Machine
*Translated by Eleanor Goodman*

**RAÚL ZURITA** Inri
*Translated by William Rowe; Preface by Norma Cole*